The child and family policy divide

Tensions, convergence and rights

Clem Henricson and Andrew Bainham

JOSEPH ROWNTREE FOUNDATION

The **Joseph Rowntree Foundation** has supported this project as part of its programme of research and innovative development projects, which it hopes will be of value to policy makers, practitioners and service users. The facts presented and views expressed in this report are, however, those of the authors and not necessarily those of the Foundation.

Joseph Rowntree Foundation, The Homestead, 40 Water End, York YO30 6WP
Website: www.jrf.org.uk

The authors

Clem Henricson is Director of Research and Policy at the National Family and Parenting Institute.

Andrew Bainham is Reader in Family Law and Policy at the University of Cambridge and a Fellow of Christ's College.

ISBN 1 85935 330 4   (paperback)
ISBN 1 85935 331 2   (pdf: available at www.jrf.org.uk)

A CIP catalogue record for this report is available from the British Library.

Cover design by Adkins Design

Prepared and printed by:
York Publishing Services Ltd
64 Hallfield Road
Layerthorpe
York
YO31 7ZQ
Tel: 01904 430033   Fax: 01904 430868   Website: www.yps-publishing.co.uk

Further copies of this report, or any other JRF publication, can be obtained either from the JRF website (www.jrf.org.uk/bookshop/) or from our distributor, York Publishing Services Ltd, at the above address.

CONTENTS

LIST OF ABBREVIATIONS

CAFCASS	Children and Family Court Advisory and Support Service
CRC	United Nations Convention on the Rights of the Child
DfES	Department for Education and Skills
ECHR	European Convention on Human Rights and Fundamental Freedoms
ECT	EC Treaty
EU	European Union
GNP	Gross national product
HRA	Human Rights Act 1998
IPPR	Institute of Public Policy Research
LEA	Local education authority
LGA	Local Government Association
NAPs	National Action Plans
NFPI	National Family and Parenting Institute
PSA	Public Service Agreement
RE	Religious education
RME	Religious and moral education
TEU	Treaty on European Union
UN	United Nations

ACKNOWLEDGEMENTS

The authors would like to thank Susan Taylor from the Joseph Rowntree Foundation and members of the project's advisory group for their invaluable support and advice: Ruth Dalzell, Barbara Hearn, the late Allan Levy QC, Mavis MacLean and Zena Peatfield. A special debt of gratitude is owed to Hannah Baker for her excellent work as research assistant to the project, and in particular for her insights into the law of the European Union. Thanks also to Maggie Jones, Pat Kneen, Carena Rogers and Sir Michael Rutter for reading and commenting on the report.

1 INTRODUCTION

There is a difficult and unresolved tension within social policy and practice in responding to the needs of children on the one hand and parents on the other; it pervades family law, government planning structures for children and parents, and almost every service associated with family life, including health, education, criminal justice, financial support and child protection. This is a tension that is imbued with a variety of ideological influences including conservatism, welfarism, social liberalism, religious perspectives and theories of children's and human rights. It is a tension that also heavily mirrors social relations, for example the growing emancipation of children, the democratisation of family relations and an evolving liberal attitude endorsing a search for fulfilment in adult relationships.

This study examines the child and family policy divide – the nature of the interests involved, its causes and consequences – and formulates possible resolutions to the policy, administrative and legal difficulties emerging in this area. It assesses the relationship between child and family policy, considering trends associated with the pivotal Children Act 1989, and assessing its consequences in the context of recent thinking and developments. One of the most significant of these is the Human Rights Act 1998 (HRA), which has major implications for family support and children's and adults' rights. Central and local government and other child welfare agencies now have to work in this new and not widely understood environment, ensuring that policies and individual actions by public authorities comply with the Act's requirements. The study looks at the child and family policy divide in the context of this and other significant national and international developments.

Policy and practice relevance

The dichotomy of child and family policy is giving rise to growing concerns in relation to the fragmentation and non-cohesive nature of services, as testified to by commentaries such as Lord Laming's from the Victoria Climbié inquiry. Laming (2003) reported multiple well-intentioned initiatives that were failing to provide synchronised support for children and their families. The National Family and Parenting Institute's (NFPI's) *National Mapping of Family Services* (Henricson *et al.*, 2001) found anxieties among local planners and service deliverers over splits between children's and family/parenting services. Many considered that planning and service delivery were hampered and that a more unified response might result in greater investment in early preventative approaches.

The Green Paper *Every Child Matters* (HM Treasury, 2003) and the Children Act 2004 set a new agenda, which looks to increasing the volume and effectiveness of services across the early preventative family support spectrum and in relation to high-risk child-protection contingencies. It establishes a Children's Commissioner responsible to a Minister for Children and Families, and multi-agency, holistically styled Children's Trusts are being piloted as local planning and delivery vehicles.

This review is particularly pertinent against a backdrop of growing international regulation of the relationship between the State, the child and the family. The incipient Children's Commissioner for England will have the duty to take into account the United Nations Convention on the Rights of the Child (CRC) with its international stipulations, safeguards and entitlements for the status of childhood. The CRC is an instrument to which the UK Government is a signatory, and, although not incorporated into domestic legislation, it is having an increasing influence on the Government's and other policy makers' and practitioners' commitment to children's perspectives.

The HRA, which effectively incorporates the European Convention on Human Rights and Fundamental Freedoms (ECHR) into English law, has a complementary – as well as potentially conflicting – role with its provision for adults and children alike of respect for their family life. Concerns have been increasingly voiced by family lawyers about a possible contradiction between the welfare principle, which makes children's interests paramount, and the commitment to the human rights of parents and other family members under the Act (Swindells *et al.*, 1999). The reappraisal of contact arrangements by the Department of Constitutional Affairs is also significant here. The bedding in of the HRA makes this a crucial time for a review of the relationship between children's and parents' interests in family law.

While anxieties have been voiced over the divide between children's and family services, some children's organisations have argued for the retention of these divisions because of the need to champion and safeguard children's interests, which have previously been eclipsed (Henricson, 2002). Arguably, there are times when the separate development of policies in relation to a specific interest offers benefits and times when amalgamation, a bringing together, offers the greatest potential for supporting different interests in society. However, even during periods of separate development, social interdependency – particularly in families, bonded as they are by a web of personal and financial relations – requires the support of government in managing separate interests so that they are mutually beneficial.

This is a highly charged and emotive area, and one where

judgements about mutual and separate interests are often difficult to make from the planning of services through to individual family interventions and contact arrangement decisions. Yet, despite the emerging concerns over these tensions, they have not been researched, or solutions sought, across the interface between social policy and families. This study aims to begin the process of addressing this deficit. It is intended to enhance understanding of the divide between children's and families' interests in social policy, and by so doing to assist national and local government to take informed decisions in relation to the management of these interests. It offers an overview and considers issues of principle.

There will always be occasions, for example in relation to child protection, when there is a potential conflict of interests between children and their parents and families, where separate policies and actions are needed. There will also be circumstances in which there is a unity of interests, for example with respect to financial support for families. The study seeks to identify those areas of public concern that require a separate approach to children and those that are better met by a unified approach to children as members of their families. Inevitably, values will have a significant part to play in determining recommendations of this nature. The standard by which judgements are made in this report is not one of endorsing the supremacy of a specific set of interests above others, nor a simple utilitarian one – the greatest happiness of the majority of family members – but rather one that has as its aim maximising the well-being of all. Within this context it is guided by the need to uphold children's rights and the human rights of all members of the family, to promote child welfare and child protection, and to accommodate separate and common interests in the family. It is intended to promote a balanced and complementary set of services across the child–family policy divide.

Method

A literature review

As a policy analysis exercise that was intended to instigate debate on the relationship between children's and family policy, the study was conducted through a review of documents across family law, education, criminal justice, child protection and financial support.

The review encompassed documentation relating to the past 20 years in order to enable a picture to emerge of the trends and issues linked to the Children Act 1989, and its consequences in the context of recent thinking and developments. There was a cut off point of October 2004. Within this time span, the review had a dual focus, first on international instruments and their scope and potential for impact, and second on the response of the current UK Government to these and other influences across child and family policy.

The documentation and associated commentaries that were considered included the following.

1   Family law reports.

2   European Union (EU) and Council of Europe
    intergovernmental documentation that has implications for
    children's, parenting and family policy in England and Wales:
    • directives
    • international conventions.

3   UK government documentation that has implications for
    children's, parenting and family policy in England and
    Wales, including:

- legislation
- strategy documents
- documents associated with the establishment of government initiatives related to child and family welfare
- ministerial speeches
- other government documentation.

The sources of the literature included specialist legal databases, research databases, bibliographic resources and the following web sites: parliamentary, official publications, UK government, individual government departments, EU, Council of Europe and children and families' networks.

Structure of the report

The report assesses the interplay between child and family policy, and the potential for governments to provide a steer that is balanced and capable of reconciling the needs of children and adults. It starts from an international perspective with consideration of the impact of individual human and children's rights promoted supranationally on approaches in the UK to managing the complementary and conflictual relationship that typifies children's and parents' interests.

Following this introduction, Chapter 2 sets the historical scene and looks at international instruments – specifically the CRC and the HRA, and policy directions in the EU. Chapter 3 moves domestic policy centre stage, probing exemplary issues on the Government's agenda to illustrate different aspects of the child–family policy divide, and the role played by international rights stipulations in the UK. In three substantive sections, there is an exploration of the Government's social inclusion and anti-poverty strategies across the life cycle; the counterclaims of early preventative family support and child protection; and the status given to children's agency and the dynamic determining the relative influence on children's outcomes of the State, parents and children themselves. There is then a section on the structures of government that relate to child and family policy, and the degree to which they underwrite a synchronised approach. The concluding chapter draws out the principal themes, points of friction and patterns of complementarity in policy adjudication. It discusses the proposition of intergenerational equality of interests as a policy yardstick. It advocates transparency – a recognition of interdependence and the conflicts that arise. It proposes a clear governmental response to the issues and moots a fuller endorsement of international rights perspectives to achieve this.

Summary

1   This report considers the tension in social policy in responding to the needs of children on the one hand and parents on the other. It does so in the context of international obligations and human and children's rights.

2   It advocates an approach that recognises divergent and complementary interests within families, and proposes ways of reconciling those interests with a view to maximising the well-being of all family members.

2 INTERNATIONAL PERSPECTIVES

International commitments

Family policy and rights

Laws and policies that affect children and families must comply with the international obligations that are imposed on the UK under a growing number of Conventions to which it is party. There has been a relentless 'internationalisation' of family law in recent decades. Although there are many Conventions that have implications for children and families, this chapter will seek to illuminate what may be required of the UK as a member of the Council of Europe bound by the ECHR (Kilkelly, 1999; Swindells *et al.*, 1999), as a member of the EU and as a party to the CRC (Le Blanc, 1999). Some of these obligations are to respect, and not unjustifiably to interfere with, the *rights* of family members, whether parents, children or other members of the family. Most obviously this is the case under the ECHR and the CRC, though only the former enables individuals to seek to enforce their rights directly before the English courts. These obligations, whether directly enforceable or not, may be either negative or positive in nature. They may either prohibit *interference* with rights or they may place the State under positive obligations to take action that is calculated to *promote* rights. A recent illustration of the State's failure to comply with positive obligations is a decision of the European Court of Human Rights involving Turkey (*Hansen* v. *Turkey* [2004] 1 FLR 142). Here Turkey was found to have breached Article 8 of the ECHR for failing to take sufficient positive measures to facilitate reunion between an Icelandic mother and her children when they had been taken to Turkey by their father.

This rights-based framework, as well as being a matter of legal obligation, may also be a useful benchmark against which to evaluate government policy. Indeed, so far as the ECHR is concerned, it is a legal obligation imposed by the HRA that the minister responsible must make a declaration of compatibility with the Convention in relation to any new bill introduced into Parliament (HRA, s. 19). What these international obligations would appear to require is an approach to social policy that is sensitive to rights within the family. It may indeed be doubted how far a social policy that conceives of child outcomes as its sole or principal objective, to the exclusion of a wider family policy, would comply with the UK's external obligations.

International commitments, however, are self-evidently not merely a matter of upholding individual rights. They are also a matter of having an input into, and complying with, the more general policies affecting families and children formulated by the Council of Europe and the EU (McGlynn, 2001a). Traditionally it has been *family policy*, rather than policies specifically directed at children, that has been the focus of attention. But, in recent years, and especially since the advent of the CRC, there has been a gathering impetus both within the Council of Europe and the EU (Stalford, 2000) to construct policies that are evaluated in terms of their impact on children, which comply with the CRC and which recognise the individual status of children. At the European level, as well as domestically, questions have arisen about the relationship between family policy and the promotion of children's rights. There is no doubt a perceptible trend towards policies that place children and their rights much higher up the political agenda, though there are those who would like to see this process carried further (Euronet, 1999). It is also clear that there are those who are less than comfortable with this major shift of emphasis. Critics have been inclined to ask where this leaves family policy and what attitude should now be taken by the State to the family in general and parents in particular (Collins *et al.*, 2002). The recent structural reorganisation, whereby family policy has been transferred to the Department for Education and Skills (DfES) under the leadership of a Minister of State primarily responsible for children, has also been called into question by one leading commentator on family law (Cretney, 2003).

Balancing rights and interests

What we seek to demonstrate in this chapter is that the key requirement is *balance*. Policies and laws affecting children and the family should be sensitive to the rights of *all* members of the family and should seek to strike an appropriate balance where they may be thought to come into conflict. Legislation and policies emanating from the Government must pay proper regard to children's rights, but they must also be balanced in the sense that they must not ignore the rights of parents and other members of the family. To conceptualise the objective of Government, wherever children's interests may be affected, purely as one of giving paramount importance to those interests, risks creating the very sort of *imbalance* that was characteristic of the period in which the emphasis was very largely on parents and families, and in which the independent interests of children received little or no recognition. In two respects we would go further and argue that the exercise may involve balancing *individual* rights or interests with *collective* rights or interests.

First, there is the question of *the family* as an entity in its own right. It may be that on occasions the individual interests of one child may conflict with the wider interests of *the family* of which that child forms a part. In such circumstances it is by no means obvious that the interests of the individual child should prevail over what might be seen as the greater good of the family unit. The Irish Constitution, for example, expressly confers rights on *the family*. Article 41.1.1 provides:

> The State recognises the Family as the natural primary and fundamental unit group of society, and as a moral institution possessing inalienable and imprescriptible rights, antecedent and superior to all positive law.

More significantly for the United Kingdom, the Charter of Fundamental Rights of the EU provides expressly that '*the family* shall enjoy legal, economic and social protection' (Article 33, our emphasis). Whether it is possible, philosophically or jurisprudentially, to conceive of *the family* as an entity capable of possessing rights is a question deserving closer attention than it has received. But the answer to this question is not in our view crucial since, even if the family is incapable of bearing *rights*, it is certainly possible to argue that it has distinctive *interests* that are deserving of respect.

If we were to consider government policy over very many decades, it is *the family* as a unit that has been considered so crucial to the well-being of society. It is *the family* that the State has been and still is so keen to support and sustain (see particularly Home Office, 1998). It is not the individual rights of its constituent members that have been at the forefront of social policy. This is not to say that support for the family as an entity is unproblematic since there has been much debate – in Parliament, in the courts and among academics – about what kinds of social groupings may properly be brought within the concept of the family. While we have seen in recent decades a distinct shift in the law away from the privileged treatment of the traditional, nuclear family based on marriage, especially in relation to the recognition of same-sex relationships (for example, the recent decision of the House of Lords in *Ghaidan* v. *Godin-Mendoza* [2004] 2 FLR 600 and the Adoption and Children Act 2002, s. 50), the overall picture is far from clear. Moreover, there appears to be a significant divergence of approach to this question within the Council of Europe and the EU. The former, in part through the judgements of the European Court of Human Rights, has been moving strongly in the direction of an inclusive approach to the question of family membership, which, for example, takes account of unconventional and same-sex relationships, whereas the latter has been much more conservative. It has been argued specifically that the European Court of Justice has failed to recognise changes in family practices across Europe and has instead adhered to a traditional view of the nuclear family within marriage (McGlynn, 2001a; Stalford, 2003).

Second, there is the question of how to balance individual rights with the wider, collective interests of *society*. There will be occasions when the promotion of the individual rights of children must give way to the public interest. This is recognised in several provisions of the Children Act 1989 (for example, s. 25 dealing with secure accommodation). Indeed, the point should be made that there are also many occasions when, even on the face of legislation, children's interests are not expressed to be paramount and are capable of being outweighed by other interests – for example, in the context of the domestic violence legislation (Family Law Act 1996, Part IV) or where a court is considering making financial orders on divorce (Matrimonial Causes Act 1973, s. 25). An additional dimension exists where the interests of more than one child in the family may conflict. The English courts have struggled with this issue, most memorably in 2000 when it was necessary to adjudicate between the interests of conjoined twins in a life and death situation (*Re A [Conjoined Twins: Medical Treatment]* [2001] 1 FLR 1).

One example of the public interest prevailing over the interests of individual parents, children and families is surely the compulsory education system. The State has decreed that all children must be educated up to the school-leaving age (Education Act 1996, s. 7). It is not open either to the parent or to the child to argue that the child should be exempt from education on the basis of that child's rights or interests, or on the basis that the State should not interfere with parental prerogatives over upbringing. It is in the interests of society that all children should be educated for at least a minimum period of time. Society also has a financial interest in the support of children, which is thought to justify a compulsory child support scheme and, at least in theory, the universal liability of parents to support their children (Child Support Act 1991 as amended). This obligation exists irrespective of whether the children themselves or their primary carers benefit directly from its enforcement. It is worth considering, then, how far the collective interests of society in matters affecting children should appropriately be allowed to trump individual rights. In the summer of 2003, two fathers successfully challenged in the courts the decision of the respective mothers *not* to arrange for their children to be immunised with the controversial MMR vaccine (*Re C [Welfare of Child: Immunisation]* [2003] 2 FLR 1054 and see Baker, 2004). It was decided that it was in the best interests of the children to receive it, even though this involved interfering with the decision of the mothers who were the primary carers. Although it was not argued in this way, it is surely not fanciful to conceive of an argument based on the collective interests of children in the community. The interests of society in the prevention of childhood diseases points towards immunisation, however the individual rights of those parents, or the welfare of those individual children, might be perceived.

The task therefore for the Government in formulating policies affecting children and families is to be aware of the different rights and interests at stake, including the independent rights and interests of parents and the public interest, and to attempt to achieve a proper balance between them. This balance needs to be struck across a range of areas including child protection, education, juvenile offending, child support, child poverty and so on. In Chapter 3, we consider how well this balance is currently being achieved by New Labour. But, first, we need to focus a little more closely on what may be required by the ECHR and the HRA, by the CRC and by membership of the EU.

The European Convention on Human Rights and Fundamental Freedoms

Convention rights and the family

Although a number of articles in the ECHR may be invoked in cases affecting children and families, it is Article 8 that is the article dealing directly with family life. Children are not specifically mentioned in the article and the Convention, more generally, is almost silent about them. This largely reflects the thinking in 1950. It is now accepted beyond doubt that children are persons under the Convention and, in the language of the HRA, that they possess 'convention rights'. Article 8 (1) provides that 'everyone has the right to respect for his private and family life, his home and his correspondence'. Article 8 (2) then prohibits the State from interfering with this right unless such interference is justified on one of the grounds set out in Article 8 (2). The right to respect for family life is therefore a *qualified* and not an absolute right; interferences by the State must be *in accordance with the law,* be *necessary* in a democratic society and *proportionate* to certain legitimate aims. These include:

> … the interests of national security, public safety or the economic well-being of the country … the prevention of disorder or crime … the protection of health or morals or … the protection of the rights and freedoms of others.

Children and parents both have convention rights. The article itself acknowledges that these may be outweighed by the public interest. So far as the family as an entity is concerned, it is at least arguable that the collective interests of the family could legitimise an interference with individual rights if held to fall within the notion of the 'rights and freedoms of others'. It is this provision that also demonstrates the *relative* nature of family rights under the Convention. Thus, interference with the rights of a parent may be justified on the basis of the child's welfare, a father's right may have to give way to the rights and interests of the mother and so on. It is a weighing process; but under this balancing exercise an approach which simply assumes that one interest or right must automatically be preferred over another is in danger of violating the Convention. That is why, even though there is now authority that suggests that the child's welfare should be preferred where it appears in the final analysis to clash with parental rights (*Yousef* v. *the Netherlands* [2003] 1 FLR 210) this is far from saying that parental rights may simply be ignored.

For this reason it has been argued that the long-established welfare principle in English law sits uncomfortably with the scheme of the Convention and may need some adaptation or redefinition (Herring, 1999; Eekelaar, 2002). The chief difficulty is that the welfare principle was authoritatively interpreted to mean that the child's interests were to be regarded as not only the court's primary or most important consideration but also the court's *sole* consideration (per Lord MacDermott in *J* v. *C* [1970] AC 668). All other claims, in particular those of parents, were thought to be subsumed in this one investigation of the child's welfare and consequently the position was widely taken, not least in the Children Act 1989 itself, that parents did not possess such a thing as *independent rights* qua parents. This view of the parental position must now be re-evaluated in the light of the ECHR. What the ECHR requires is that parents' rights and interests be balanced with those of the child, with the child's rights and interests playing a *preponderant* role but not an exclusive one.

Child protection

In the area of child protection we can see how the ECHR requires the State to engage in a most sensitive balancing exercise. The ECHR has massive implications for the way in which local authorities conduct themselves in performing their statutory role and for the allocation of their resources.

On the one hand, Article 3 of the ECHR provides that 'No one shall be subjected to torture or to inhuman or degrading treatment or punishment'. This has been interpreted by the European Court of Human Rights to include situations in which children have been abused or neglected. Where the evidence is that proper intervention by the local authority might have prevented its occurrence, it is now established that in certain circumstances it may be liable in damages for negligence or breach of statutory duty. Moreover, a breach of Article 3 may be established where an authority is aware that children are suffering abuse and fails to take sufficient steps to protect them (*Z* v. *United Kingdom* [2001] 2 FLR 612 and *TP and KM* v. *United Kingdom* [2001] 2 FLR 549).

On the other hand, it is equally clear that over-zealous intervention by the authority may also give rise to a breach of the ECHR. The key point is that proportionality requires that the authority take only such action as is *necessary* to safeguard the child's welfare. There is a massive emphasis in the jurisprudence of the European Court of Human Rights on reunification of parent and child where it has proved necessary for a child to be temporarily looked after by the State (see especially *Johansen* v. *Norway* [1996] 23 EHRR 33). Breaches of the ECHR are likely to occur where insufficient steps are taken to maintain contact between the child and the family, and where there has been a failure to work sufficiently hard to achieve reunification (*S and G* v. *Italy* [2000] 2 FLR 771). The essence of what the ECHR requires is that a strong priority be given to supporting the family and the child's position in that family. There is also a very strong requirement that parents should be allowed to participate properly at every stage of care procedures, as an aspect of Article 6, which protects the right of everyone to 'a fair and public hearing' in the determination of their civil rights and obligations (*P, C and S* v. *United Kingdom* [2002] 2 FLR 631). There is much speculation about whether the public law regime of the Children Act 1989 can survive future challenge in so far as it fails to afford parents the opportunity to continue to be heard on all significant matters relating to children in care.

The obligations under the ECHR in relation to child protection therefore have the potential to pull local authorities in two separate directions. On the one hand, they must devote enough resources to protect children seriously at risk, but, on the other hand, they must commit extensive resources to family support and to working with parents to reunite them with children temporarily looked after by the State. How this balance of resource allocation is struck, already an extremely difficult question for cash-strapped authorities, has become an even more acute problem with the potential for human rights violations if they get it wrong. And, increasingly, the courts are unlikely to be excessively sympathetic to the argument that local authorities were unable to make the provision visualised by the legislation for the sole reason of being under-resourced (see, for example, *R. v. Sefton MBC Ex p Help the Aged and Others* [1997] 4 All ER 532; *R. v. East Sussex CC Ex p Tandy* [1998] AC 714; *R. v. Birmingham City Council Ex p Mohammed* [1999] 1 WLR 33; cf. *R. v. Gloucestershire CC and Another Ex p Barry* [1997] AC 584). Perhaps there is a case here for greater transparency in priorities and for central Government to give stronger guidance to local authorities in relation to appropriate allocations of resources between family support and protection of children at risk.

Adoption

The case law of the European Court of Human Rights has established violations of the ECHR on many occasions, in the UK and in other countries, where there has been insufficient attention paid to parents' rights. Another context in which the danger of neglecting parental rights is all too clear is that of adoption. Traditionally, adoption law has attached more weight to parental wishes than in most other areas of legal disputes concerning children. Thus, until recently, it was axiomatic that the welfare or best interests of the child were *not* paramount when it came to deciding whether an adoption order could be granted in the face of opposition by the parent. The principal ground relied on for dispensing with parental consent was that a parent was withholding consent unreasonably (Adoption Act 1976, s. 16). There were a significant number of cases in which the objection of the parent to adoption was upheld on the basis that the parent was not withholding consent unreasonably despite a professional view favouring adoption on welfare grounds (see especially *Re M [Adoption and Residence Order]* [1998] 1 FLR 570 and *Re B [Adoption Order]* [2001] 2 FLR 26). This safeguard of the parental position has been removed at a stroke by the new Adoption and

Children Act 2002, which makes the welfare of the child the *paramount* consideration throughout adoption proceedings and extends to the parent's decision to withhold consent (s. 52 [1]). The change in the law is part of a wider change of policy direction by the Government, signalled in the White Paper that preceded the Act (Department of Health, 2000a) and a review by the Performance and Innovation Unit (Cabinet Office, 2000), which favours adoption as the solution to the position of children looked after by local authorities on a long-term basis. Whether such an approach, which is not favoured by certain other European countries and which is not supported by conclusive evidence that adoption is a better long-term solution for children than alternative solutions (Warman and Roberts, 2003), is compatible with the requirements of the ECHR is open to considerable doubt. It is not, for example, immediately apparent that government-imposed targets for increasing adoption figures are consistent with the notion that local authorities should be doing everything they are able to do to keep the child in the birth family and to achieve reunification. Other European countries, such as France, the Netherlands and Sweden, devote a much higher proportion of their resources to family support and reunification, and hardly resort at all to domestic adoption for children looked after by the State (Warman and Roberts, 2003).

Family support

It may be that the area of child protection and adoption is one in which there is a danger in focusing attention entirely on the interests or rights of the child and forgetting that the child's rights are first and foremost protected by support for *the family*. This was recently acknowledged by Lord Laming who concluded:

> It is not possible to separate the protection of children from the wider support to families. Indeed often the best protection for a child is achieved by the timely intervention of family support services ... the needs of a child and his/her family are often inseparable.
>
> (Laming, 2003)

We acknowledge that an essential aspect of the advancement of children's rights has been the gradual recognition of their independent interests and an identity separate from that of their parents. Nowhere has this been more apparent than in their separate representation in public law proceedings where parents were previously allowed to represent their children in the very proceedings in which they themselves might be facing allegations of abuse or neglect. It was not until the Children Act 1975 that separate representation for children in care proceedings was introduced. The appreciation of the potential conflicts of interest that may exist within the family is without doubt central to an understanding of individual rights. But it does not follow from this that interests within the family will always conflict since it is clearly the case that individual rights are best upheld in many cases by support for the family unit as a whole through, for example, an adequate supply of social housing, an effective health service and social security system. This we would argue is recognised in many articles of the CRC; ostensibly a Convention concerned only with the rights of children but in reality much concerned with the adoption by states of an effective family policy as the best means of protecting children's rights.

In considering what may be required of states under international obligations, therefore, one important objective is surely to establish those areas in which there is a potential *conflict of interest* between the child and other members of the family and those areas in which there is a *common interest*. Quite clearly the protection of children's rights requires separate children-oriented policies, structures and laws where there is an apparent conflict of interest but, equally clearly, a properly thought out family policy may serve the interests of children better where there is no such conflict. It is for this reason that we find the notion that all policies affecting children must be directed to the single objective of giving prime importance to children's rights or welfare unsatisfactory and unhelpful. It is an approach that might, if it resulted in an undervaluing of the rights of other family members, lead to violations of the ECHR.

The United Nations Convention on the Rights of the Child

Protecting children's rights in the family

The CRC is self-evidently about children and about the promotion of children's rights. It is the most wide-ranging and widely ratified international instrument of its kind. It would be possible to conclude rather quickly from this that the CRC is about states adopting child-centred policies and that children, as opposed to families, are its only concern. On a closer examination, however, it is clear that the CRC is also about the importance of parents and the family to children and this is explicitly recognised in many of its provisions. The following are just some of the more obvious provisions and are intended only as illustrations. Article 3(2) requires state parties to undertake to:

> ... ensure the child such protection and care as is necessary for his or her well-being, *taking into account the rights and duties of his or her parents, legal guardians, or other individuals legally responsible for him or her.*
>
> (Our emphasis)

21

LIB

Article 5 requires state parties to:

> ... *respect the responsibilities, rights and duties of parents or, where applicable, the members of the extended family or community as provided for by local custom, legal guardians or other persons legally responsible for the child*, to provide, in a manner consistent with the evolving capacities of the child, appropriate direction and guidance in the exercise by the child of the rights recognised in the present Convention.
>
> (Our emphasis)

These articles support the primary role of parents in raising children, a principle that is reflected throughout the Convention. The role of the family, more specifically, is expressly emphasised in the Preamble to the CRC, which reiterates that state parties are:

> Convinced that the family, as the fundamental group of society and the natural environment for the growth and well-being of its members and particularly children, should be afforded the necessary protection and assistance so that it can fully assume its responsibilities within the community.

And further:

> Recognizing that the child, for the full and harmonious development of his or her personality, should grow up in a family environment, in an atmosphere of happiness, love and understanding.

None of this is to deny the importance of the individual rights of the child, but what these provisions make clear is that the child's rights are first and foremost protected within the context of the family and by the State giving proper support to families. There is nothing in the CRC that lends support to the notion that states should abandon or dilute family policy in pursuit of a purely child-centred social policy, which regards the interests and rights of children in isolation or detachment from those of the families of which children form a part.

UN Committee reports – a failure of family policy or a failure of children's policy?

The performance of states under the CRC is monitored and is the subject of periodic reports by the UN Committee on the Rights of the Child (CRC Part II, Articles 42–5). In reading the reports that relate to the United Kingdom's performance under the CRC, it is perhaps fair to ask whether the failings identified in these reports are the result of policies that fail to take sufficient account of the individual rights or interests of children, or the result of a failure to have a sufficiently effective family policy. In its report on the UK in October 2002 the Committee was, for example, critical of the UK's failure to deal with the problem of child poverty (United Nations, 2002). While the Committee welcomed the Government's commitment to eliminate child poverty and the initiatives it had taken in this respect, it considered that more could be done. It commented on 'the lack of an effective and coordinated poverty eradication strategy across the state party'. In order to address concerns over children's living standards, it is clearly arguable that a substantial component of government policy should be an eradication of poverty across the board within the families and households to which those children belong. Another criticism of the report was the imperfect rights that children have regarding knowledge of their biological parents (paras 31 and 32); ostensibly an assertion of the independent rights of children, but in reality recognition of the importance to children of establishing and fostering familial links.

Other failings identified by the Committee, in contrast, would clearly appear to be the result of the State giving inadequate recognition to children as individuals capable of possessing independent rights. These include the absence of procedural rights, such as the right to be heard before being excluded from school and the right to appeal against exclusion (paras 47 and 48). They also include rights of recipience such as the right to health education, especially sex education, and access to confidential and adolescent-sensitive advice or information.

The European Union

The family and the European Union

Neither children nor families have been much mentioned in the major treaties of the EU (Rome, Maastricht, Amsterdam and Nice). This is not altogether surprising given the 'economic' roots of the EU. The treaties provide no legal basis for the development of a family law and indeed it had been held by the European Court of Justice some 20 years ago that the EU had no jurisdiction regarding the 'organisation of family life' (Case 184/83 *Hofmann* v. *Barmer Ersatzkasse* [1984] ECR 3047, para. 24). Notwithstanding this lack of formal legal competence, EU law and policy has had a certain impact on member states' regulation of the family, whether through the definition of 'family member' for the purposes of the free movement of workers or through secondary legislation regulating parental leave or the provision of childcare. Recognising this, the institutions of the EU have been developing a 'family policy' (McGlynn, 2001a). In the early 1980s, the EU Parliament advocated the adoption of a 'comprehensive family policy', which would encourage member states to take account of the needs of families when introducing legislation and, where appropriate, harmonise policies at Community level (Resolution on Family Policy in the EC [1983] OJ C184/116). More recently, in 1999, the Parliament called on member states to 'conduct specific family policies supporting and protecting the family financially and its role as an educational force' and 'to take account in their policy of the needs and requirements of families' (Resolution on the Protection of Families and Children [1999] OJ C128/79, No. 3). The Commission and Council largely endorsed this approach (European Commission Communication, Family Policies COM [98] 363; Conclusions of the Council and of the Ministers Responsible for Family Affairs [1989] OJ C277/2). The impact of these statements in member states is limited, however, because of their non-binding nature. In 2001, McGlynn (2001b) concluded that, in so far as Community law and policy regulates families, it does so 'in a piecemeal, ad hoc fashion and largely as an adjunct to other policy areas'.

The absence of a legal basis enabling EU legislation in matters of substantive family law has not, however, prevented the recent enactment of a number of EU regulations on the recognition and enforcement of judgements in family matters (Council Regulation No. 44/2001 with regard to maintenance obligations; Council Regulation No. 1347/2000 [so-called 'Brussels II'], soon to be replaced by Regulation No. 2201/2003 [so-called 'Brussels II bis'] with regard to matrimonial matters and parental responsibility). In 1999, judgements in the field of family litigation were identified by the Tampere European Council as needing to be 'automatically recognised throughout the Union without any intermediate proceedings or grounds for refusal of enforcement' (Tampere European Council Conclusions [point 34], October 1999). Such private international law measures, nominally in pursuit of economic aims, were also responding 'to the frequently expressed concerns of [the] citizens' (Tampere European Council). Free movement provisions had had a noticeable impact on European family life and there was an acceptance within the EU that legal regulation in the resulting cross-border family support, in terms of easy 'access to justice' for the 'cross-border family', is seen as increasingly crucial; and the Regulations implementing this, binding in their entirety and directly applicable in all member states, mandate the states to act accordingly.

The future of the family and family policy within the EU is a matter of speculation but it could consist of an ever-increasing Union influence in our family life. First, the new EU Constitution could have a significant impact in the family field. The draft European Constitutional Treaty with amendments was agreed by EU leaders on 18 June 2004 but will now need to be ratified by member states. If it is, the European Charter of Fundamental Rights, which was 'solemnly Proclaimed' by the EU institutions in 2000 and which forms Part II of the new Constitution, will become legally binding on member states. The Charter explicitly includes 'family provisions' and it has been observed by McGlynn (2001b) that the focus is on 'the family' as a unit to be protected by the European Union in its own right and not merely to be exploited in the pursuit of other goals. She also notes that Article 16 of the European Social Charter gives protection to families as do the Constitutions of a number of member states. The German Constitution, for example, states that 'marriage and the family shall enjoy the special protection of the state' and we noted above the protection of the family under the Irish Constitution.

These 'family provisions' of the Charter will become hard legal norms and states may face legal challenges where they fail to abide by them. Articles such as Article 33 (1), declaring that 'the family shall enjoy legal, economic and social protection' could become very significant. Of course the Charter itself is explicit that it is not to have the effect of extending community competence (Article 51 [2]) and accordingly it will apply to member states *only when implementing EU law.* However, if community competence continues to expand, the UK may increasingly have to abide by the Charter provisions. Moreover, the policies emanating from the EU institutions themselves will be required to be evaluated in terms of their likely impact on the family. This may raise questions about how far the UK could adopt child-centred legislation or policies without considering the likely effect of these measures on the family as a whole.

Children and the European Union

While the EU has been vocal in its support of families, it has been said that children are largely invisible in EU law. In so far as children's interests were considered at all in the law and policies of the EU, this was largely as an adjunct to other aims and in association with policies affecting parents and families. In that sense the claims of children, in so far as they could be said to be recognised at all, were 'parasitic' in nature. Children were regarded as appendices of parent 'workers' rather than as 'European citizens' in their own right (McGlynn, 2001a). A useful comparison may obviously be made here with the very different approach of the Council of Europe and the appreciation that children are persons capable of possessing 'convention rights' for the purposes of the ECHR (Kilkelly, 1999). Notwithstanding the lack of a legal status for children in EU treaties, it has been observed that the EU had adopted an impressive catalogue of measures that affected children indirectly, albeit as the product of a highly fragmented policy. Such measures related to family policy, custody and kidnapping, migrants within the community, immigrants and refugees from outside the community, poverty, education, day care, sexual exploitation, the media, children with disabilities, the exchange of young people, toy safety, protection against accidents in the home, youth unemployment and adoption. What has so far been lacking is a 'co-ordinating structure for developing and streamlining a coherent and comprehensive children's rights policy' (Council of Europe, Social, Health and Family Affairs Committee, 'Building a 21st century society with and for children': follow-up to the European Strategy for Children, Recommendation 1286, 1996, para. 50).

The first direct reference to children in EU treaties came with the amendments to the EC Treaty (ECT) and the Treaty on European Union (TEU) introduced by the Treaty of Amsterdam in 1997. These amendments included a number of articles that had as their aim the protection of children in relation to such matters as the prohibition of discrimination based on age in Article 13 (ECT), Article 137 (ECT) on social exclusion (which could be used also in relation to children) and the amendment to Article K.1 (now Article 29 TEU), concerned with trafficking offences against children. A further reference to children was introduced with the 'solemn proclamation' of the European Charter of Fundamental Rights. This heralded in a number of provisions acknowledging, directly or indirectly, the interests and rights of children as individuals. Article 24, for example, reproduces some of the central features of the CRC. Article 24 (2) states that: 'In all actions relating to children, whether taken by public authorities or private institutions, the child's best interests must be a primary consideration'. Furthermore, Articles 20 and 21, indirectly at least, also recognise the child as a bearer of rights and carry the implication that EU policy must be 'child proof' in the sense that it must not openly discriminate between children and adults without good cause and that in principle all Charter rights extend to children. Thus, Article 20 provides that: 'Everyone is equal before the law' and is situated in a chapter that goes on to set out the rights of the child along with the rights of other vulnerable groups such as the disabled and older people. Article 21 prohibits discrimination on a number of grounds, of which age is one. The cumulative effect of these provisions may be to usher in a new kind of thinking about children in EU law as individual citizens capable of bearing rights (McGlynn, 2001b; see also Stalford, 2000).These rights, especially as set out in Article 24, reflect the familiar balance in the CRC and elsewhere (for example in the Children Act 1989) between the right of the child to receive various forms of protection and the right to limited autonomy and self-expression.

McGlynn (2001b) notes that, under the CRC, the child's best interests are expressed to be only 'a primary' consideration and not, as in the Children Act 1989, 'the paramount' consideration. The implication of this of course is that other interests may outweigh the interests of individual children affected by particular actions, most obviously for present purposes the interests of parents or the wider family. But she goes further than this to draw attention to what she sees as a specific concern surrounding this formula in the EU context. She notes that the wording was the result of a compromise after lengthy debate in which the conclusion was that 'justice and society at large should be of at least equal, if not greater, importance than the interests of the child' (McGlynn, 2001b). This is in the context of a wider criticism that the European Court of Justice has been rather too inclined to prefer the economic or commercial interests of the EU over those of the human rights under consideration. It has been argued, for example, that this has been so in relation to the Distance Selling Directive and toy and TV advertising policies of the EU. Another way of looking at the formula under Article 24 is that, in bringing into play other interests that may compete with and conceivably outweigh the interests of individual children, it may be permissible, or even necessary, within the EU to pay as much attention to policies affecting the family as to those affecting children more specifically.

Despite the direct acknowledgement of children's rights and interest in the Charter, many advocates of children's rights feel that it could have gone further. The most vocal of these is Euronet, a European organisation that is campaigning for greater rights for children within the EU. Among its more significant demands are that the Charter should have contained an explicit reference to the CRC and indeed that respect for the principles and standards of the CRC should be incorporated into EU law. It also argues that, in tackling child poverty and social exclusion within the EU, the interests of children, who are particularly vulnerable to both, should be treated separately and disaggregated from the more general needs of parents and families (Ruxton and Bennett, 2002). Perhaps most importantly, it argues for the development within the EU of children's policies that it believes to be needed alongside a family policy (Euronet, 1999). One palpable success of the lobbying by Euronet is the direct reference to children's rights in the new European Constitution. Article 3 sets out the objectives of the European Union, one of which is to 'contribute to ... protection of human rights and *in particular children's rights*' (Article 3 [4], our emphasis). It will be interesting to see if this 'singling out' of children's rights leads to a more child-focused EU family policy once the Constitution is in force, or whether such a reference will simply be taken as a constitutional guarantee of the principles contained in the ECHR and the EU Charter; that is that the human rights of everyone within the family must be taken into account when formulating law and policy, but, when such rights conflict, primary or 'particular' consideration should be given to the interests of the child (see *Yousef* v. *the Netherlands* for this principle in ECHR jurisprudence). With the requirement of the EU's accession to the ECHR once the new Constitution is in force (Article I-7 (2), Draft Constitution) and the explicit adoption of the ECHR fundamental rights as 'general principles' of EU law (Article I-7 (3), Draft Constitution), the latter interpretation is perhaps the more likely. Member states may then find themselves constitutionally bound to carry out the balancing exercise proposed here when formulating law and policy in the family arena.

Concluding remarks

In this chapter we have sought to demonstrate that the UK's principal international obligations in relation to the family require it to have both an effective family policy and a distinctive policy protecting the rights and interests of children. There is no doubt that, at one time, there was an unwillingness to recognise and provide for the independent interests and rights of children. The story of the acceptance of the notion of children's rights is very largely one of gradual recognition of their independent status as juristic persons and not mere adjuncts of their parents or constituent members of a family. However, we believe that it would be equally inappropriate for the pendulum to swing so far in the opposite direction that government policy in relation to families should be focused *entirely on children*, their rights and their best interests. Whether we look at the ECHR (with its emphasis on achieving a sensitive balance between often-competing rights), or the CRC (with its open support for the principle that children's rights are best protected by state support for the family), or the EU (which clearly has a long-standing interest in the family and is only now beginning to think about a children policy), it is clear that the UK needs to maintain its commitment to families as well as to children.

The real question we believe is one of balance and ensuring that policies supporting families and children are complementary. Government policies affect children, parents and families in very many ways, both directly and indirectly. What needs to be evaluated in each case is whether the policy in question sufficiently well accommodates these separate and sometimes competing interests. It has often been said, for example, that education law in the UK is entirely concerned with the status of parents, their preferences, rights and duties, to the almost total neglect of the independent rights or interests of children who, after all, are those most directly affected by education law and policy. Conversely, the Government's policy on openly pushing adoption as the long-term solution for children looked after by the State may be criticised as paying scant regard to the fundamental rights of parents and to reunification of the child with the birth family wherever practically feasible. In the following chapter we focus our attention on how well New Labour is achieving this balance at a time of structural reorganisation of the services for children and families.

Summary

International commitments
1 The UK's policies affecting children and families need to comply with the obligations imposed by international conventions. These obligations may be either positive or negative in nature.

2 Policies must be balanced and take into account the rights of all individual members of the family as well as the collective interests of families and the wider public interest.

The European Convention on Human Rights
1 The ECHR gives to parents, children and other members of the family 'convention rights', which the UK is required to respect and which may be enforced directly in the courts by virtue of the Human Rights Act 1998.

(Continued)

2   Interference with these rights is allowable only in accordance with the limited justifications laid down in the ECHR.

3   Child protection policies should be adequate to protect children from 'torture, inhuman and degrading treatment' under Article 3 but must also, under Article 8, give a strong priority to family support services and reunification of the child with the natural family. Careful consideration needs to be given to the balance of resources committed to these dual objectives, which can pull in opposite directions.

4   Policies relating to adoption need to be sensitive to both children and parents' fundamental right to respect for their family life.

The United Nations Convention on the Rights of the Child

1   The CRC asserts the independent rights of children over a wide range of issues but also acknowledges in many of its articles that children's rights are most effectively protected by policies that support the family.

2   The periodic reports of the UN Committee on the Rights of the Child indicate the ways in which the UK is failing to comply with its obligations under the Convention. These failings may reflect either inadequate recognition of the individual rights of children or an ineffective family policy.

The European Union

1   The European Union has traditionally lacked competence to legislate directly in the field of family law but, recognising the impact of the EU's economic policies, especially that relating to the free movement of persons, it has been developing a family policy.

(Continued overleaf)

2   As and when the new EU Constitution is ratified by member states, the European Charter of Fundamental Rights will become legally binding on them. The Charter explicitly provides that the family shall enjoy the special protection of the State.

3   Children were originally considered in EU law only as appendices of their parents, who in turn featured primarily as workers. More recently the EU has adopted a range of measures affecting children more directly. The European Charter of Fundamental Rights expressly recognises the rights and interests of children. The new European Constitution also explicitly sets out that it is one of the objectives of the EU to contribute to the protection of children's rights.

Concluding remarks

1   International obligations would seem to require the UK to have *both* a family policy and a distinctive policy protecting the rights and interests of children.

2   Such policies should be balanced and complementary so that they accommodate the separate and sometimes competing rights and interests within the family.

3 THE UK DIMENSION

Introduction

In this chapter we apply the litmus test of balance and complementary approaches to the UK Government's record on supporting child and family interests. We probe into its responses in an environment of increasing international legislative direction in the context of three determining influences: the UN, the EU and the Council of Europe. And we do this in a country that has eschewed family policy per se. The nearest the UK has come to a family policy has been in this Government's commitment to *Supporting Families* (Home Office, 1998) – a strategy statement, now somewhat out of date. But policies have mushroomed across the domain that might fall within the purview of family policy.

This is a government that has shown a preoccupation with supporting child rearing as part of its social inclusion strategy, its war on anti-social behaviour and, more broadly, as part of a communitarian and humanistic philosophy entailing an overarching concern with fostering positive human relations. It has shown an interest, albeit with a lower profile, in personal relationships that go beyond child rearing per se, embracing an interest in cementing personal and supportive relationships across the age spectrum. A concurrent subsidiary line in the Government's thinking has been 'rights', but, as we shall see, this has been cast within a strictly limited conceptual framework, around civil rather than social rights, and even in relation to civil rights there is some straining at the leash.

Philosophies aside, a driving force in government policy has been process. How can the Government enhance service delivery on the ground? How can it ensure that the failures in service competence that led to Victoria Climbié's death are, if not eradicated, at least ameliorated? The degree to which process anxieties have contributed to a holistic approach to families and children also emerges from our exploration.

We examine substantial areas of government policy where the interplay of child and family interests and associated policies throw up significant exemplary issues. They include anti-poverty strategies, which have been core to the Government's social policy objectives; child protection and the pervasive tussle between early preventative and reactive hard-end responses; and relative voices in the eternal triangle of alliances between State, child and parents across education, family law and youth justice. Finally, there is the role of government structures in all of this. How does the broad sweep of government direction and mechanisms facilitate or thwart the achievement of balance in handling child, parent and family interests?

Poverty and the life cycle

Here we look at the emotive issue of poverty and the thinking behind its redress. Combating social inequality is a core governmental function undertaken for humanitarian reasons and to preserve the social fabric and cohesion of the State. In broaching the relationship between child and family policies, the question arises as to how these endeavours should spread across the population age span. Is there a common obligation to all age groups? Should investment be led by prevailing poverty levels, or vulnerability, or the potential for making a long-term impact on individual lives and in reducing the intergenerational cycle of disadvantage – or a combination of these? They are all pertinent and not always compatible considerations in making investment decisions, and they are laden with moral and practical dimensions. We examine whether under the current Government there has been a move from the redistribution of wealth on behalf of the population as a whole in favour of the elimination of child poverty, and the arguments underwriting and countering any such shift.

From a human rights perspective, there are issues around whether the Government should be focusing on child or all poverty. From a children's rights perspective, it has to be asked whether one can split addressing the poverty of the family from children's poverty; where does the differentiation lie, unless, of course, the child has left home and is de facto independent? And, critically in the world of real politic, it has to be posited that child poverty may have become the acceptable face of redistribution and that this may be leading the Government in its responses.

Supranational influences

The external stipulations and pointers, to which administrations may have regard in determining policies in this area, exist, but are perhaps insufficiently defined given the centrality of poverty to government activity. Certainly the balance between emphasis on adult, family and child poverty is not fully explored in European and UN instruments.

There are, as we have seen, EU and Council of Europe recommendations and directives that place expectations on member states to address social exclusion. There is also specific reference to family poverty. An obvious example is the Council of Europe directive on Coherent and Integrated Family Policies, which exhorts governments to promote family economic autonomy and to take into account the costs of child rearing. But it is the CRC that is perhaps the international document most clearly geared to child poverty. Here the focus is on family material well-being for the purpose of enhancing child outcomes; concerns over other family members in their own right are not the issue in this instrument. However, it would be fair to say that there is relatively little anticipation in the CRC of circumstances requiring differentiation of children's material support needs from their family context.

The CRC's limited statement is perhaps fleshed out and should be read in the context of the wider discourse that has arisen in association with its children's rights perspective. For example, Marshall (2003) makes the case for tackling childhood poverty as a separate phenomenon requiring child-tailored solutions. She contends that poverty experienced in childhood takes place during a stage in life that is critical for the development of the whole human being:

> While childhood poverty shares causes and manifestations with poverty experienced by adults, there are some important different causes and effects. Crucially, childhood poverty may have lifelong consequences.
>
> (Marshall, 2003)

Poverty in childhood can deny someone opportunities that affect the rest of their life. Furthermore, children are vulnerable, dependent and still growing. Significantly there are issues around access to resources within a household; children, or children of one gender, or an individual child may be excluded or their child-centred needs not met. Consequently reducing family poverty may not necessarily be coterminous with promoting children's well-being (Marshall, 2003).

On behalf of Euronet, Ruxton and Bennett (2002) consider childhood poverty from a rights perspective within the European

Union administration. Broadly concurring with the rationale put forward by Marshall for addressing child poverty separately, they draw on the CRC's commitment to children's rights to protection, provision and participation. Particular reliance is placed on Article 4, which requires governments to invest 'the maximum resources available' for the promotion of children and young people's economic, social and cultural rights. They develop this and the CRC's Article 12, which establishes children's right to participate actively in society and decision making, to formulate recommendations for child-specific poverty indicators. These include receipt and management of income within families and significant material redistribution over the family life cycle and between those with and without children. However, no quantifiable recommendation is made in respect of this income differentiation and no guidance given in terms of the proportion of gross national product to be ideally spent on children.

The UK Government and social exclusion

The UK Government has a broad agenda on social exclusion. Julian Le Grand *et al.* (2005, in progress), in their ongoing programme of research into policies and concepts of material deprivation, describe the Labour Government as having had a comprehensive 'war on poverty', albeit that it has not been marketed as such. A range of measures have been undertaken to counter poverty in childhood and old age, and against individual and area social exclusion.

As part of EU administrative integration, the UK Government, together with other member states, has produced a National Action Plan on Social Inclusion – most recently for 2003–05 (Department of Work and Pensions, 2003a) – which has the broad sweep of social inclusion and exclusion issues within its purview. Targeted groups at significant risk of social exclusion include, as well as children, large families, ethnic minorities, disabled and older people – and key risks: living in a jobless household; living with persistent low income; living in a deprived community; and intergenerational poverty. There is clear evidence that the Government's action across this broad spectrum of interests and concerns is having an impact. For example, we have witnessed a reduction in elder poverty, with some 1.2 million having been raised above the poverty line between 1997 and 2003/04 (Sutherland *et al.*, 2003).

The Government's projection of its anti-poverty strategy is nevertheless dominated by child poverty reduction targets. It is child poverty that is the lead issue in ministerial statements on social exclusion. Tony Blair, in setting out the future of the welfare state under New Labour, described 'our historic aim that ours is the first generation to end child poverty forever, and it will take a generation. It is a 20 year mission but I believe it can be done' (Blair, 1999, p. 7).

> Child poverty is a scar on Britain's soul. It is simply unacceptable that millions of children should start their lives in families where no one works or where they are caught in the poverty trap, in poor housing, under-nourished and condemned to substandard education and healthcare. That is why Tony Blair has said we will not rest until we have banished child poverty from the face of Britain.
>
> (Brown, 1999, p. 8)

More recently, in 2004, the Treasury held a seminar for sociologists, economists and other social reformers on investment measures to enhance social mobility, which presupposes the preferential claims of the early stages of people's development, as these are most likely to influence upward mobility. And it is child poverty that predominates in the preamble and discussion in strategy documents such as the National Action Plan on Social Inclusion, and it is clearly established as the Government's primary social exclusion target in Opportunities for All with its regular progress reports.

In terms of secured outcomes and achievements, too, there has been a radical reduction in child poverty, which suggests its core aim status in government thinking. The Institute of Fiscal Studies has shown that, since 1999, support for families with children has grown by 52 per cent in real terms, and suggests that between 10 and 25 per cent of parents with children receive more government financial support than the estimated cost of their children (Adam and Brewer, 2004). Analysing the Family Resources Survey, Sutherland et al. (2003) show that, between 1996/97 and 2000/01, there was considerable poverty reduction in respect of children but less in relation to other groups. This is attributed largely to benefits for groups without children falling relative to incomes generally – for example those on Job Seeker's Allowance, Incapacity Benefit and Income Support if living without children. Countering this trend, there has been a considerable hike in pensioner income since 2001 with the introduction of the pension credit, but the thrust of government redistribution policies is still slanted towards addressing children's needs.

> Whereas in 1997 Britain's child poverty record was placed amongst the worst in Europe, I am clear that in order to achieve our ambitions we must strive towards being amongst the best.
>
> (Department of Work and Pensions, 2003b)

There have been complaints by organisations such as End Child Poverty (2003) over the failure of the Government to make greater inroads into children's relative deprivation. Particular concerns have been expressed over the abandonment by the Department of Work and Pensions (2003b) of the goal of ending child poverty by 2020 and replacing it with the goal of achieving one of the lowest child poverty levels in Europe. It is certainly the case that, with average incomes having grown significantly since 1996/97, the relative poverty line has shifted to such a degree that fewer children have been lifted out of relative deprivation than had been anticipated. Nevertheless, it is broadly acknowledged in academic analysis that the Government has had substantial success in reducing child poverty however defined – whether in absolute or even relative terms (Brewer *et al.*, 2002; Sutherland *et al.*, 2003). Indeed, Sutherland and colleagues predict that the Government's intention of reducing child poverty by a quarter by 2004 will in all probability be met. This calculation includes taking housing costs into consideration; if housing costs are left out of the equation, a reduction of one third is predicted.

Family support and child outcomes

While the reduction of child poverty is the Government's principal social exclusion goal, in the event, much of its activity entails support for the wider family in anticipation of enhanced child outcomes. Support for the child is channelled through the family. This is clearly the case with fiscal policy; tax credits and benefits are directed through parents. Even the 'baby bond', a capital asset entitlement for children at birth provided by the Child Trust Fund, is not accessible by young people until they are 18.

The Education Maintenance Allowance paid directly to disadvantaged young people to help them stay in education post 16 is an exception here, and there are, of course, supports in kind targeted directly at children that impact on poverty. Education and health are the obvious cases in point and, while these are long established services, the current Government's investment in their enhancement is significant. There are also examples of new initiatives that reach children independently of their parents. There has been an expansion of personal, social and health education in schools and pilots have been conducted in schools to provide health advice and contraception directly to children on a confidential basis. Connexions has been established, which provides personal development and advice, support and opportunities directly to children aged 13–19 to help them overcome barriers to participation in learning and work.

In balancing these two approaches to supporting children – reaching children directly or by family proxy – the Government's response appears to have been largely pragmatic. While evidence has been cited that parents do pass the financial support they receive onto their children, there is perhaps insufficient discussion of children's agency or ways of improving the material benefits that actually reach children. There might, for example, be some benefit to be gained from considering a range of options for direct provision in schools that go beyond the offering of a piece of fruit for younger pupils and means-tested school lunches of dubious nutritional value. There has been debate within government departments about the provision of sexual health and contraceptive services directly to children, but this has not been run in tandem with consideration across the board of the relationship between targeting children directly and the role of the family as a conduit of support. It may be that, in the final analysis, the current balance of these different forms of support is appropriate in terms of optimising children's outcomes, or it may be that a shift is required. A strategic statement setting out the rationale and evidence for decisions in this area might increase the likelihood of an effective balance being achieved.

Rights obligations and external regulation

The Government's commitment to eradicating child poverty is arguably the sphere in which it has most readily and fully addressed its obligations under the CRC. And, although the UN Committee on the Rights of the Child in its response to the second periodic report on progress in the UK (2002) specified work to be done in relation to resource allocation, and educational disadvantage in particular, it did recognise the Government's determined stance highlighting:

> ... the national objective to halve child poverty by 2010 and eradicate it within a generation; and the strategies and policies tackling child poverty and social exclusion through locally targeted services for children.

It might be said, however, that, despite these aspirations, the Government is promoting children's 'welfare' rather than 'rights' in its social exclusion strategies. Certainly, it makes scant reference to children's rights as a concept or to international frameworks such as the CRC. There is no reference to either in the anti-poverty strategies described in *Every Child Matters* (HM Treasury, 2003), an absence sufficiently conspicuous to give rise to the following concern voiced by the House of Lords and House of Commons Joint Committee on Human Rights (2003):

> Likewise the Green Paper, a substantial programme for improving services for children, neither refers to the UN Convention nor to the Government's obligations to implement its provisions.

While a rights approach and UN-stipulated entitlements are not demonstrably part of the Government's thinking, there is a closer identification with EU economic co-ordinating activities, which lie at the heart of the Union. The *United Kingdom National Action Plan on Social Inclusion 2003–05* (Department of Work and Pensions, 2003a) is a case in point, where, along with other member states, in accordance with the Lisbon agreement, the Government has set out its strategy on social inclusion:

> We all want to make Europe the most dynamic economy in the world by 2010. With more and better jobs leading to greater social inclusion and less poverty in a way that is recognisable to people in local communities, not just in terms of official statistics.
>
> The development of National Action Plans helps support that agenda, primarily by facilitating practical co-ordination between the Member States, for example by providing the building blocks towards peer review, exchanges of best practices and so on.
>
> (Department of Work and Pensions, 2003a)

Significantly, while the importance of EU co-ordination is extolled in this report and the importance of enhanced opportunities and protection, particularly for children, there is no reference to CRC rights imperatives. Neither is social inclusiveness framed in terms of a human right across the age spectrum. Rights in any form do not yet appear to have been fully integrated into the Government's vocabulary in combating poverty.

Reconciliation of child and family interests

The arguments supporting the Government's prioritisation of child poverty are formidable. The UK had one of the highest rates in Europe when the Labour administration came to power (Ruxton and Bennett, 2002). It is also understandable that child poverty might be championed as the acceptable face of economic redistribution. In addition to these two factors, there may be an in-principle argument to be made in favour of weighting social inclusion investment towards the age in life that is likely to derive the greatest long-term benefit from it, with 'benefit' defined here in terms of impact on lifetime and intergenerational poverty. With these interlinked arguments, what is perhaps needed is in-depth discussion of the background, principles and policies relating to differentiated investment across age groups. This would provide the opportunity for the development of societal values that set childhood in the context of a lifetime's needs. It would give some transparency to the difficult choices that have to be made and enable a strategy that embraces both a recognition of those choices and the need for their making to be guided by a set of well-aired and understood principles to be pursued.

This open debate and resolution is a precondition of the Government being able to respond in any meaningful way to the CRC's Article 4, which requires support for children to the maximum of resource availability. It is not just a question of tracking the resources that are allocated to redressing childhood poverty, as implied by the UN Committee on the Rights of the Child (2002):

> The Committee recommends that the State party ensure transparent analysis of sectoral and total budgets across the State party and in the devolved administrations to show the proportion spent on children, to identify priorities

and to allocate resources to the 'maximum extent of available resources'.

It is also critically a matter of establishing how resources should be allocated between generations. And for this the CRC has no blueprint; it has no definitive statement as to how the stipulation 'maximum extent of available resources' is to be judged. In the absence of external guidance, it falls to the UK national Government to develop a benchmark.

There is also an absence in the CRC of guidance in respect of the relationship and balance between direct support for the child and support for children via their families. Here, too, it is down to the UK Government, and it would clearly be desirous for the relative effectiveness and interplay of the two forms of investment to be investigated in terms of their potential to impact on child outcomes in this country.

Family support and child protection

The relationship between, on the one hand, the Government's investment in supporting the family as a whole – early prevention and supporting the larger net of families in need – and, on the other, its investment in targeting children at risk is a fraught one. From the welfare approaches of the Children Act 1989 to the rights stipulations of the HRA and the CRC, the Government is beset by messages on these issues that in some circumstances can be viewed as contradictory. As we have seen, emphasis on the family, its preservation, the entitlement of its individual members – adults as well as children – to a family life and to due legal process can at times sit uncomfortably with expectations of the State to intervene where children require protection from their families.

In addressing this dichotomy and the potential for contradictory positions to be steered towards balanced and complementary approaches, there are two significant questions to be posed.

1 Is there a recognition of the need for balance and complementarity in terms of:
   • government investment in support services
   • the structures used to deliver those services?

2 In its moves in this direction, are child outcomes in essence the only ones being sought by the Government – with the focus being principally about developing optimum service models to achieve this, for example promoting a balance between preventative and targeted responses? Or is the Government concerned with wider rights' obligations to support individuals within the family, adults as well as children, and even the family as a collective unit, encompassing the host of civil liberties and protection claims that comprise human rights?

The protection of children and supporting their upbringing has been the subject of substantial government activity, from issuing the strategy statement *Supporting Families* (Home Office, 1998) and the introduction of the *Framework for the Assessment of Children in Need and their Families* (Department of Health, 2000b) and the Quality Protects programme during the early years of its administration, through to the establishment of the Laming inquiry into the death of Victoria Climbié and the all-embracing proposals for children and family services in the recent Green Paper *Every Child Matters* (HM Treasury, 2003), now enacted in the Children Act 2004. The challenge is whether, among this plethora of policies, we can detect a significant, consistent thread indicating the Government's position in reconciling child protection and family support.

Service investment

> The Committee is deeply concerned that between one and two children die every week as a result of violence and neglect in the home. It is also concerned at the high prevalence of violence, including sexual violence, throughout the State party, against children within families, in schools, in institutions, in the care system and in detention. It also notes with deep concern growing levels of child neglect.
> (UN Committee on the Rights of the Child, 2002)

By and large the UK Government shares these concerns of the UN Committee on the Rights of the Child:

> Sadly, nothing can ever absolutely guarantee that no child will ever be at risk again from abuse and violence from within their own family. But we all desperately want to see people, practices and policies in place to make sure that the risk is as small as is humanly possible. I believe that the proposals we are putting forward here constitute a significant step towards this goal.
> (HM Treasury, 2003, Tony Blair's Foreword)

Whatever balance has been struck in service investment, there can be no doubt in general of the Government's commitment to protecting children at risk. The introduction of Quality Protects, with its umbrella programme designed to ensure better standards in children's social services and for the upbringing of children in care, is witness to that. It encompasses the *Framework for the*

Assessment of Children in Need and their Families (Department of Health, 2000b); primarily targeted at children at risk, this instrument is intended to improve assessments and service access. On another tack, *Every Child Matters* (HM Treasury, 2003) takes forward Laming's proposal for establishing 'information, referral and tracking' procedures to enhance the capacity of welfare agencies to detect, exchange information and act on indicators of children being at risk at the earliest opportunity. *Every Child Matters* is a broad strategy statement, but detailed practice recommendations have also been produced in a linked publication *Keeping Children Safe* (Department for Education and Skills *et al.*, 2003).

Unspecified in publicly available documents, the cost of the Government's new child protection measures, from support services to data collection and information exchange arrangements, may be judged on any estimate to be substantial. However, this commitment notwithstanding, the Government's investment in new early preventative programmes with a family support dimension is probably greater. Sure Start, for example, is an ambitious programme to promote the physical, intellectual and social development of babies and young children in areas of social deprivation. The core of the programme offered includes a visit to all new parents introducing them to Sure Start services, enhanced childcare, play and early learning opportunities, better access to health services and a range of parenting courses and groups. The Government's aspiration in *Every Child Matters* is to roll out Sure Start from its currently geographically restricted base. New investment across preventative services such as Extended Schools, the Parenting and Children's Funds, Home Start, helplines and parent information sessions in schools, all of which cater for families, is major, and to this should be added the preventative thrust of taxation and welfare benefit changes introduced as part of the Government's campaign to combat child poverty.

Broadly based preventative measures are inevitably costly because of the spread of their target population; comparative analysis of investment with child protection targeted approaches is consequently difficult. What are perhaps more indicative of trends in government thinking are the many strategy statements that accompany new initiatives. Government rhetoric, in its non-pejorative sense, suggests a distinctive move towards early prevention. The very publication of *Supporting Families* (Home Office, 1998) during the first year of New Labour taking office is symptomatic of this shift with its prospectus for expanding family services.

Since then the Laming inquiry and other significant lobbyists, such as the Local Government Association (LGA) and the National Family and Parenting Institute (NFPI), have drawn the Government's attention to the significance of early preventative universal responses. In their submission to Government, *Serving Children Well – A New Vision for Services for Children*, the LGA *et al.* (2003) pressed for a balanced package but rooted in universal services for all children:

> A strategy is needed for all children: therefore any strategy for children at risk should derive from a strategy for all children.
>
> (LGA *et al.*, 2003)

The paper recommends effective support for families and children that can lead to early intervention when problems arise, and effective child-friendly alternatives when children are no longer able to live with their families.

NFPI's *The Future for Family Services* (Henricson, 2002) called for an extension of nationally stipulated preliminary universal support, including pre- and post-natal support, a pivotal health visitors' role in respect of children of all ages and information sessions about parenting for parents at key stages in their children's development, together with a menu that goes beyond this initial provision, offering a range of services that are appropriate to the different levels and nature of individual families' support requirements.

The Government for its part has demonstrated similar aspirations. In its Spending Review (2002) it reviewed its investment in early preventative services since *Supporting Families* (Home Office, 1998) and noted the achievement of programmes such as Sure Start and the Children Fund in supporting families. The Review's recommendations emphasised the need to focus on preventative services and to broaden the reach of provision through mainstreaming. Presaging the Green Paper *Every Child Matters* (HM Treasury, 2003), Paul Boateng (2003), Chief Secretary to the Treasury, set out the Government's intention to go beyond a procedural response to child protection issues to address the span of services involving all children. The Minister stressed that 'at risk' would be interpreted in its widest sense to include children who are failing to achieve their potential, who have a range of vulnerabilities and disabilities, who suffer multiple discrimination and who are at risk of abuse or violence. In the event, *Every Child Matters* went further than this. It emphasised the critical role of universal services in the context of which child protection would sit:

> We need to ensure we properly protect children at risk within a framework of universal services which support every child to develop their full potential and which aim to prevent negative outcomes ... As Lord Laming's recommendations made clear, child protection cannot be separated from policies to improve children's lives as a

whole. We need to focus both on the universal services which every child uses, and on more targeted services for those with additional needs. The policies set out in the Green Paper are designed both to protect children and maximise their potential. It sets out a framework for services that cover children and young people from birth to 19 living in England.

(HM Treasury, 2003)

As proposed in *The Future for Family Services* (Henricson, 2002), *Every Child Matters* sets out a bedrock of universal provision coupled with a range of services for specific issues. Multidisciplinary teams are proposed in and around schools and children's centres to provide a rapid response to need. The emphasis is on providing support tailored to families' requirements. And the document is expansive about the Government's intention to support parents and families with a chapter of proposals on 'Supporting parents and carers', which opens with this declaration:

In the past public policy has paid insufficient attention to supporting parents and helping families find solutions for themselves. By bringing policy on parenting and family support into the Department for Education and Skills, alongside policy on children, the Government has put it at the heart of children's services.

(HM Treasury, 2003)

The Government credits its pursuit of a preventative approach with having achieved a reduction in the numbers of children on the child protection register:

... numbers on the child protection register have been falling. At 31 March 2002 there were 25,700. Ten years previously the numbers were 38,600.

(HM Treasury, 2003)

Service structures

Moving from service investment to service structures – recent changes here are indicative of an administrative perspective that does not view child protection in remedial isolation requiring a different response to the 'normal' family and the support activities that typify the State's relationship with families and children as a whole.

Laming (2003) resisted calls from the Institute of Public Policy Research (IPPR) for a separate, dedicated child protection service, divorced from mainstream local government social service facilities. He took the view, concurring with the LGA *et al.* (2003), that families and children move in and out of risk, often over long periods of time, and that the separation of child protection and family support would be virtually impossible. Concerns were expressed that a separate national child protection agency would jeopardise any possibility of a continuum of family support and would not improve outcomes for either children or families.

Laming, and subsequently the Government in *Every Child Matters* (HM Treasury, 2003), not only eschewed the separation route, but also promoted greater integration through structural reorganisation nationally and locally. At the national level, child protection has been brought from the Department of Health to sit alongside family support in the Department for Education and Skills, family support having been moved from its former berth in the Home Office. Locally, Children's Trusts are being created as a co-operative body encompassing the full range of services for children and families in a local authority area.

Integration of child protection and family support is a radical governmental shift, and it can be seen not only in overarching administrative structures but also in early intervention mechanisms. 'Information exchange, referral and tracking' as proposed by both Laming and the Government is not a narrow device targeting child protection cases; it is conceived as a broad point of reference and data resource on children and families to enable support to be offered in relation to a multiplicity of problems and issues. Whether a data collection instrument of such all-embracing dimensions should be introduced is debatable, but the espousal of integration is nevertheless demonstrated by its conception.

Integration can be seen, yet again, with proposals for a 'common assessment tool', which would enable professionals working with families – teachers, medical staff, social workers, etc. – to produce interchangeable assessment measures and documentation. This represents an expansion of the standardisation in the *Framework for the Assessment of Children in Need* (Department of Health, 2000b), introduced at the beginning of the Government's term in office, with its exclusive focus on children whose vulnerability places them at risk.

From one perspective, the move towards joined-up administration can be traced to a trend in current child protection policy towards supporting children in the context of their families. Keeping the family together and supporting it to this end is preferred to taking children into care. From express advocacy of this principle in the Children Act, to its affirmation in both the *Framework for the Assessment of Children in Need* (Department of Health, 2000b) and the *Integrated Children's System* (Department of Health, 2002), there can be little doubt that the balance in official child protection guidance favours keeping families together. With its remit to support children in need, and in particular those at risk of serious harm, the *Framework for the*

Assessment of Children in Need notes the need for social workers to attend to the requirements of the family as a whole:

> Social services, in their assessment of whether a child is in need and how to respond to those needs, also have to take into consideration other children in the family and the general circumstances of that family. Social services have to identify the impact of what is happening to the child and also the likely impact of any intervention on that child and on other family members.
>
> (Department of Health, 2000b)

Generally, it can be said that this perspective of family preservation prevails despite social work anxieties over repercussions when things go wrong and periodic swings towards a greater readiness to remove children into local authority protection (Campion, 1995).

Rights obligations and external regulation

In its development of family support and child protection, the Government appears to be taking some note of the CRC and the HRA. For example, the 'information, referral and tracking' proposals in *Every Child Matters*, albeit mediated through Lord Laming's report, stem from a recommendation by the UN Committee on the Rights of the Child. The establishment of a Children's Commissioner, who will have some overview of child protection and support, has similar origins.

The House of Lords and House of Commons Joint Committee on Human Rights (2003) welcomed a number of proposals in *Every Child Matters* that address concerns raised by the UN Committee on the Rights of the Child (2002) in its report on the implementation of the CRC in the UK. Examples include expansion of child and adolescent mental health services, improving the education of children in care, measures to tackle bullying and continued commitment to reduce child poverty. There is, however, relatively little government documentation in this field that makes specific reference to compliance with rights stipulations – external or otherwise. The *Framework for the Assessment for Children in Need* (Department of Health, 2000b) draws attention to the significance of the CRC and the HRA, but does not specify the details of its compliance with these instruments, its sole acknowledgement being:

> The Guidance describes the Assessment Framework and the Government's expectations of how it will be used. It reflects the principles contained within the United Nations Convention on the Rights of the Child, ratified by the UK Government in 1991 and the Human Rights Act 1989.
> (Department of Health, 2000b)

Every Child Matters makes scant overt reference to human and children's rights obligations. In terms of overarching aims, it is solely concerned with child outcomes and makes no concession to the independent entitlements of parents and families, in particular under Articles 6 and 8 of the ECHR. There is no discussion of the human right entitlement to respect for family life, which European case law has construed as implying that children should be removed from their family only as a last resort. While we have seen that in practice this approach is largely followed, a strategic document of this nature should have made reference to such basic human entitlements. And there are other significant provisions that go unremarked, such as participatory rights – significantly, parents' right to make their views known in relation to dealings with their children.

This absence of a family-wide rights perspective may have led the Government, in hard-end social care cases involving adoption, to promote legislation which arguably pays insufficient regard to the fundamental rights of parents to respect for their family life. Exclusive emphasis on child outcomes may be undermining the Government's interest in supporting other family members, once it has been determined that the birth family context is not conducive to promoting the child's best interests.[1] As we have seen in Chapter 2, the Adoption and Children Act 2002 can be criticised as failing to take sufficient account of the fundamental interest that both parent and child have in preservation of their family relationship in law. Where adoption is sought in the face of a parent's objection, the former test of whether that parent was withholding consent unreasonably (the primary test under the Adoption Act 1976) has been replaced by a straightforward child welfare test. This change goes against the recommendations of the Adoption Review of the 1990s (Department of Health and Welsh Office, 1992), which favoured a test that would have required it to be demonstrated that adoption was better than any alternative solution. Furthermore, post-adoption contact with the birth family, which might have been officially encouraged as an aspect of 'open adoption', has been left largely to the courts' discretion. The implied policy here of driving up adoption figures is questionable in the context of the expectations associated with the ECHR, which are to provide family support for children in difficulty and, where children are in care, to make strenuous efforts at their reunification with their birth parents.

Reconciliation of child and family interests

In summary, the Government appears to recognise its obligations to improve child protection procedures, including identifying children when they are at risk more effectively than has been undertaken hitherto. It also recognises an obligation to support the family bond by offering both early preventative and early intervention facilities and support to sustain families when children are at risk. In its discussion of the issues in documents such as *Supporting Families* (Home Office, 1998) and *Every Child Matters* (HM Treasury, 2003), the Government demonstrably appreciates that there is a balance to be struck between family support and child protection, and that integration and complementary responses are essential rather than segregated professional slants and service options.

What it perhaps fails to specify in quantifiable terms are the optimum levels relative to each other of investment in early prevention, early intervention, family support in at-risk cases and local authority care. The task would undoubtedly be difficult. There would, for example, be a need to take into account differing locality profiles. But responsibility for decisions should not be ducked because of their complexity. Currently, local authorities are left with the task of allocating resources and, where these are limited, are likely to focus on reactive fire fighting, protecting themselves from culpability in failing to prevent serious harm to children. Directives on investment levels would probably be resisted in the current climate of national–local government relations; national specifications are increasingly focused on outcomes rather than process, with the latter left to local discretion. But, given the sensitivity of child protection, some open government discussion in concrete financial terms of relative investment expectations may be helpful. It may also be critical in response to decisions of the European Court implicitly requiring a balance of investment between child protection and family support, reflecting the requirement of Article 3 of the ECHR concerning freedom from inhuman and degrading treatment and Article 8 requiring respect for family life (see discussion in Chapter 2).

While investment guidance is limited, legal and procedural requirements of professionals abound. And they are on the increase following the Laming report. Do they distort or appropriately guide investment decisions? The legal differentiation in the Children Act 1989 between s. 17 cases (children in need) and s. 47 cases (children at risk of serious harm), with the latter involving a legal requirement on the local authority to instigate investigations, compared with less closely defined obligations for children in need, will probably continue to weight local investment in favour of hard-end child protection responses. Critics of the child protection system in the UK suggest that a highly regulated, process-driven service, determined by the fear of legal consequences, is suppressing professional creativity in supporting children and families who are at risk (Moss and Petrie, 2002; Cooper *et al.*, 2003).

Leeway for some, if limited, professional risk taking, coupled with an indication of preferred relative investment patterns across early and intermediate family support and hard-end protection, are perhaps preconditions for ensuring the fruition of the Government's interest in promoting early responses and family preservation options. This clearly has to be done in the context of resource availability. A request by both the Association of Directors of Social Services and the House of Commons Select Committee on Health (2003) for a review of the relationship between demand and resources available for social care might provide an opportunity to probe these issues.

Rights issues

The Committee is also concerned at the absence of a global vision of children's rights and its translation into a national plan of action ... The Committee encourages the State party to incorporate into domestic law the rights,

principles and provisions of the Convention to ensure compliance of all legislation with the Convention, a more widespread application of the provisions and principles of the Convention in legal and administrative proceedings, and a better dissemination and training of the Convention.
(UN Committee on the Rights of the Child, 2002)

This commentary from the UN Committee on the Rights of the Child reports the failure of the UK to adopt fully a children's rights ethos and to integrate the CRC into its children's policy, with spin-offs for both family support and child protection. While a Children's Commissioner is to be introduced and training offered to professionals in the CRC, generally, the terms in which *Every Child Matters* is cast suggest that this rights deficit in service and political rationale and determination may be set to continue (House of Lords and House of Commons Joint Committee on Human Rights, 2003). Informal discussions about the role of the Children's Commissioner also indicate a remit concerned with children's outcomes, but not children's rights.

While children's welfare is at the heart of *Every Child Matters*, the absence of a rights perspective ducks the issue of entitlement of children and parents to any of the services on offer[2] and the issue of external regulation. Not only are children's rights missing, but also human rights. This is highly significant in respect of the relationship between supporting families and protecting children. It allows a focus on child outcomes to be pursued without reference to the entitlements of other household members. And yet, as we have seen in Chapter 2, these entitlements, for example to respect for family life and to due legal process in child protection cases, exist underwritten not only by Council of Europe and UN expectations, but also in the UK by the HRA. There needs, perhaps, to be greater cognisance in strategic government thinking, evidenced in its public statements and discussion documents, of the human rights dimension to be addressed in decisions about family support, child protection and social care decisions, all of which impinge on access to a family life. Failure to do this may result in two systems of thinking emerging that may not be wholly compatible – one in the legal sphere linked to international institutions and associated case law, and the other in the family and children's policy generated by the British Government.

Self-determination and protection: the child and the State

The scope of children's agency, including children's participation in decisions that affect their lives, their entitlement to services as individuals independent of their families and even a say in their running, has developed steadily over generations supported by human rights' advocates and social welfare reformers. And, in recent years, it has grown with marked rapidity, partly as a result of judicial decisions. For example, *Gillick* v. *West Norfolk and Wisbech Area Health Authority* [1986] 1 AC 112 established a degree of independent autonomy for older adolescents in respect of contraceptive advice given by medical practitioners; the 'Gillick' case now informs health practice. It has also been typified by the promotion of the CRC with its tenets establishing children's rights of self-determination and participation. Significant aspects of this shift in childhood towards self-determination have been fostered by a protective State and are, indeed, dependent on statutory intervention supported by the judiciary. Inevitably, this has impacted on the parent–child relationship. It is a trend that circumscribes parent power in favour of the child–State axis.

Of course, there are critical societal influences that are not directly under the influence of Government contributing to changing power relations in families. Peer pressure, the decline of deference, the potency of the media and marketing, even the earlier onset of adolescence – all are contributing to strain on the umbilical cord. But, in this publication, we are looking at the role of Government in promoting children as independent human beings – and it is not insignificant; it is a role that has pertained throughout the twentieth century linked to welfare concerns, for example in the provision of health and education. And it is one that latterly has become augmented as the concept of children's rights has arrived to challenge received welfare approaches.

The arguments supporting children's rights and the importance of maximising young people's agency are not disputed here. Provisions such as Article 12 in the CRC are endorsed:

> State Parties shall assure to the child who is capable of forming his or her own views the right to express those views freely in all matters affecting the child, the views of the child being given due weight in accordance with the age and maturity of the child.

> For this purpose, the child shall in particular be provided the opportunity to be heard in any judicial and administrative proceedings affecting the child.

The question that needs to be borne in mind, however, is whether parents' authority in relation to their children is being maintained sufficiently intact to encourage them, the parents, to shoulder willingly the caring responsibilities that are expected of them. Are there also circumstances where the UK Government is promoting the child's perspective to such a degree that parents' personal interests are being unduly eclipsed? In this section we look at the balance of child and family interests, and consider in some key areas whether the shift towards children's agency has gone too far or not far enough. We examine parental separation, education and criminal justice.

Choosing residence and contact

The CRC and the ECHR both bolster children's right to be heard in circumstances where their parents are exercising their entitlement to live separately from each other. Article 12 of the CRC gives the child the right to a say over his or her destiny and Articles 6 and 8 of the ECHR accord any individual, children included, the right to respect for family life and a fair hearing, implying access to due legal process. Against this backdrop of international rights, what progress has been made in putting the child's voice centre stage in deciding with whom s/he should reside and have contact? The indications are that there has been considerable movement in this direction and that the Government is at least in step with, if not in the vanguard of, developments.

The legal context in which children's views are being increasingly considered is one where there is no statutory presumption of contact as such; the Children Act 1989 provides that the child's welfare is the overriding consideration. However, the Act encourages both parents to share in their children's upbringing after separation and case law suggests a strong presumption of contact:

> ... the courts naturally start with the view that in most cases contact between the child and the non-resident parent is desirable both for the child and the parent.
> (Butler-Sloss, 2001)

Current government policy has underwritten this stance through the creation of a Public Service Agreement (PSA) target in 2002 by the then Lord Chancellor's Department of increasing contact where it is safe and in the interests of the child. The thrust of the Government's aim is described as:

> … to enable children to benefit from the stability offered by a loving relationship with both parents, even if they separate.
>
> (Lord Chancellor's Department, 2002)

More recently, the Green Paper *Parental Separation: Children's Needs and Parents' Responsibilities* (Department for Constitutional Affairs *et al.*, 2004) reaffirms the Government's position in the following terms:

> The Government firmly believes that, in the event of parental separation, a child's welfare is best promoted by a continuing relationship with both parents, as long as it is safe to do so.
>
> (Department for Constitutional Affairs *et al.*, 2004)

Children's welfare is established as the determining factor here, but this is in the context of a presumption that that welfare is best served by contact, with no indication that children's views should be the critical determinant.

There has nevertheless been in recent years a movement towards consulting children, which can be attributed to a combination of a greater appreciation of its value in achieving optimum welfare outcomes and a growing recognition of children's rights. The Government is cognisant of a volume of new research that points to the benefits of involving children in post-separation decisions, as well as concerns over parental pressure and manipulation (O'Quigley, 1999; Hunt, 2003; Hunt and Roberts, 2004).

The Children and Family Court Advisory and Support Service (CAFCASS) staff are expected to elicit children's views in producing their reports in contested court hearings. Significantly, in terms of the external regulation of children's rights, CAFCASS in its draft guidance for court officers cites the CRC stipulations that children be heard. The Adoption and Children Act 2002, is also likely to increase the incidence of children's interests being represented by a guardian or solicitor.

In uncontested cases, the Government has promoted the use of 'parenting plans', which stress the importance of involving children. Guidance to post-separation settlement mediators and publicly funded solicitors anticipates the encouragement of parents to consult their children.

While promising steps have been taken, there are options for consideration that would further increase the likelihood and scope of child consultation. These have been flagged up by Hunt and Roberts (2004) as including, as well as the enhancement of services provided directly to children, such as information, advice, consultation and advocacy, some legal stipulations including requirements that:

- parents take account of their children's views, as under the Children (Scotland) Act 1995

- courts ascertain the children's views before granting divorce

- children have legal representation – this may be particularly pertinent where there is a possible conflict of interest.

We have witnessed some measurable shift towards according children rights of hearing in and out of court complying with the specifications of the CRC and HRA. This has not, perhaps, been matched by a commensurate recognition of adults' entitlements, in particular the entitlement of parents to enjoy the society of their children under the family life provisions of the HRA. While separated parents' right to be heard in relation to divorce or other proceedings has been long established, and there are clear presumptions that contact benefits children, adults' human rights entitlement to respect for family life has generally been understated. And there is no evidence of a significant change in government stance over this, although the vociferous fathers' lobby may be beginning to have an impact. The Green Paper *Parental Separation: Children's Needs and Parents' Responsibilities* (Department for Constitutional Affairs *et al.*, 2004) does refer to the HRA:

> The Human Rights Act 1998 also requires the courts to interpret the law (including the Children Act 1989) in a way that is consistent with the European Convention on Human Rights. Article 8 of the Convention requires respect for private and family life. This includes respect for the rights of both parents who enjoy life with their children to have contact with those children, provided this is consistent with the welfare of the children, and also the rights of children to have beneficial relationships with their parents. The proposals in this consultation document reflect the Government's commitment to its Convention responsibilities to families.
> (Department for Constitutional Affairs *et al.*, 2004)

However, this is introduced as something of an adjunct in a paper that does not otherwise refer to parental rights as such and has the following principal and repeated aim:

> The law, as set out in the Children Act 1989, makes clear
> that the welfare of the child is the paramount
> consideration in any court decision concerning a child's
> upbringing. The Government believes that this principle
> should be sustained without qualification, in order that
> there continues to be the clearest possible focus on the
> needs of children.
>
> (Department for Constitutional Affairs *et al.*, 2004)

The issue is whether the child welfare principle should stand alone when contact and residence decisions are made, or whether it should be considered in conjunction with, albeit superseding, a parent's entitlement to respect for family life. Arguably the latter offers a more open and balanced recognition of the multiple interests – children and adults — that exist within families and require reconciliation. And the weight of international requirements certainly endorses this approach.

The international conventions make it plain that contact is a *right* of both children and parents. The State must take reasonable steps to enforce contact orders made by the courts, despite many suggestions by commentators to the contrary, as a matter of international obligation. This has been consistently held by the European Court of Human Rights (see, for example, *Hokkanen* v. *Finland* [1996] 1 FLR 289; *Ignaccolo-Zenide* v. *Romania* [2001] 31 EHRR 7; *Glaser* v. *United Kingdom* [2001] 1 FLR 153; and, most recently, *Kosmopoulou* v. *Greece* [2004] 1 FLR 800). Violations of the ECHR for failure to make sufficient efforts to sustain contact are every bit as much about violating the rights of the parent as they are about violating the rights of the child.

The Council of Europe's new Convention on Contact Concerning Children 2003 is more directly explicit about the State's obligations in this respect. Article 4 of the Convention provides expressly that: 'A child *and his or her parents* shall have the right to obtain and maintain regular contact with each other' (our emphasis). It goes on to provide that: 'such contact may be restricted or excluded only where necessary in the best interests of the child'. The Explanatory Report to the Convention sets out the limited circumstances under which the State is permitted to restrict or terminate contact. The right of contact may 'only be restricted or excluded on serious grounds in the best interests of the child (e.g. as a measure necessary to protect the morals or the health of the child, etc.)' (Explanatory Report, para 8). Article 7 goes on to require judicial authorities, when resolving disputes concerning contact, 'to ensure that both parents are informed of the importance for their child *and for both of them* of establishing and maintaining regular contact with their child' (our emphasis). The Explanatory Report then sets out the thinking behind this provision:

> It aims at making parents realise that Article 4 of the present Convention contains a *fundamental right* (of the child *and his or her parents*) to obtain and develop regular contact between their child and themselves.
> (Explanatory Report, para. 58, our emphasis)

All of this is a far cry from the view, frequently voiced in England (even in Government), that contact is a right of the child but not the parent. Although the UK has not yet signed or ratified the Convention, it may be expected to do so in due course. In the light of the Convention, it will become extremely difficult to justify an official policy that has as its base the assumption that the only objective is to promote the best interests or rights of children. Rather, in order to be consistent with international obligations that recognise the independent rights of parents, the objective of court decisions and mediation in determining contact should be to assist parents in reaching an arrangement for the *maximisation* of contact with both parents within the practicalities of the individual case. The vulnerability of the child and the child's need for a stable home environment will remain the overriding concern. And there will of course be some cases, characterised by domestic violence or abuse, where the fundamental rights to contact should legitimately be displaced by the principle of the best interests of the child. But rights for all parties to contact with each other is the starting point and this should be clearly acknowledged.

Rights and education

> No person shall be denied the right to education. In the exercise of any functions which it assumes in relation to education and to teaching, the state shall respect the right of parents to ensure such education and teaching is in conformity with their own religious and philosophical convictions.
>
> (ECHR, Protocol 1, Article 2: Education)

This one stipulation in the ECHR encapsulates some of the predicaments in the tussle over parents' and the State's role in educating children. Education, laden as it is with values and torn obligations between the public and private face of bringing up children, is perhaps the sphere that illustrates most starkly the potential for child and parental interests to diverge. And it is where the State–child protective axis comes most demonstrably into play.

It is in education that the State takes over a significant parental function – that of inducting a child into the community, or at least a substantial part of that function. As Archard (2003) puts it:

> ... the state has a role as parens patriae to protect the interests of children and a further distinct interest in ensuring that any current generation of children become society's future functioning adults. The state must thus ensure that children are educated to a certain minimum extent so that they can act as citizens.
>
> (Archard, 2003, p. 119)

But parents also have a significant role, and not just a residuary one, in guiding their children's upbringing. In Scotland it has been enshrined in legislation. The Children (Scotland) Act 1995 provides that parents have a responsibility and corresponding right to:

- safeguard and promote the child's health, development and welfare until the child reaches 16

- provide direction until the child reaches 16 and guidance until the child reaches 18.

And they have, from the ECHR, and arguably from commonsensical analysis, a role – even entitlement – to set norms of living and interaction that stretch from behaviour management to spirituality.

What occurs then when, in the context of education, the interests of the child diverge from the parent? How is that interest identified and what is the role of the State in protecting it? And, in all this talk of interests, what place is there for the voice of the child? What should be its determining influence? These matters are complicated, embracing a minefield of emotions.

Making any assessment of the Government's balancing of the issues necessitates some exploration of the principles behind the notion of the best interests of the child – however contentious and slippery. A further associated concern that cannot be eliminated from the balancing act is that of the wider community, notwithstanding that it elides with the interests of both child and parent.

Children's interests

Those arguing the moral dimensions of the State's locus in children's education cite the importance of ensuring that its citizens can function as active participants in a democracy and are able to engage in the market of work, and in financial and social relations (Gutman, 1987; Rawls, 1993). Beyond this, there are arguments that, in a liberal society, children are entitled to an 'open future', one where they are equipped to make choices across cultural, spiritual and economic spheres, and to be offered, so far as possible, equality of opportunity (Coleman, 1998; de Wizje, 1999).

Those propagating choices do not suggest these are realisable only in a vacuum of moral guidance, but rather argue for some synergy between offering children a cultural, moral and spiritual framework for development, and equipping them with a capacity to criticise that framework and a knowledge of alternatives (Archard, 2003).

From the premise that the State has a legitimate aim to promote liberal democracy and the social welfare of its citizens, the questions to be asked are what protection do children's interests require in terms of education? And what are the circumstances in which parents' interests might diverge from that protective goal? Significant players here are, first, parental negligence or insufficient engagement to support the child in his/ her education and, second, counter-conviction, for example a religious belief that a particular faith should be taught exclusively or a belief that moral guidance is being incorrectly or inadequately accommodated. Religious and sex education are significant flashpoints in relation to the latter. In assessing government policy, we have to consider how well it is engaging parents in this project of education, and how well it is juggling the need to support a child's open future and views alongside parents' concerns to guide children's behaviour and thinking in accordance with their own beliefs.

International governance

International stipulation has something to say here but does not provide detailed guidance. The draft EU Constitution follows earlier human rights trends in emphasising a child's entitlement to education and it takes the UK's HRA a stage further through including a provision for free compulsory education.

The issue of securing open futures for children through this entitlement is not specifically addressed, nor is the tension between parental wishes and those of the State. The Constitution merely provides that, within member states:

> ... the right of parents to ensure the education and teaching of their children in conformity with their religious, philosophical and pedagogical convictions shall be respected.

However, the limitations of the exercise of this right is reflected in the phrase:

> ... in accordance with the national laws governing the exercise of such freedom and right.
> (European Communities, 2003, Article 11-14, Right to Education)

Drew's (2000) interpretation of parents' right to ensure that the education of their child is in conformity with their own religious and philosophical convictions in the context of the HRA suggests that the State would not intervene with education being provided from a minority perspective unless:

> ... to do so would foreclose the child's options later in life, affect the child's health and safety or amount to a breach of another right.
>
> (Drew 2000, p. 41)

There is also a provision in the CRC for children's right to freedom of thought and religion:

> State Parties shall respect the right of the child to freedom of thought, conscience and religion.

> State Parties shall respect the rights and duties of the parents and, when applicable, legal guardians, to provide direction to the child in the exercise of his or her right in a manner consistent with the evolving capacities of the child.
>
> (CRC, 1989, Article 14)

Marginally then, one can say that 'open futures' win. But, significantly, the child's voice does not. Drew (2000) concludes that the parental right as defined here would override children's own wishes.

Things may, of course, have moved on since this interpretation was given, and it is certainly worth bearing in mind the increasing emphasis that has been given to according children a say in their life course. The EU Constitution states the currently received expectation:

> Children shall have the right to such protection and care
> as is necessary for their well being. They may express
> their views freely. Such views shall be taken into
> consideration on matters which concern them in
> accordance with their age and maturity.
> (European Communities, 2003, Article 11-24)

The UN Committee on the Rights of the Child takes this bald statement further and places a great deal of weight on the child's voice determining the direction and implementation of education:

> ... ensure that legislation throughout the State party
> reflects article 12 and respects children's rights to express
> their views and have them given due weight in all matters
> concerning their education, including school discipline.
> (UN Committee on the Rights of the Child, 2002, p. 12)

Government's position

Where does the UK Government sit in this morally contentious area? Has it brought parents with it in the education of children and, in its efforts to do so, has it been able to offer children open futures and equality of opportunity sufficient to enable them to operate as effective, participating and critical agents in modern society? And has it given children a sufficient voice?

Partnership with parents

One can say with little hesitation that the Government has courted parents in relation to education, actively drawing them into the loop. Parents have some limited measure of choice, although not a right, in respect of the school to which they send children and, with a degree of transparency, league table measures offer parents information on which they can base that choice. The

Education Act 1996 requires that local education authorities (LEAs) have regard to the general principle that pupils should be educated in accordance with their parents' wishes, so far as this is compatible with addressing matters of efficiency and cost. Other resources have also been developed to provide parents with a fuller picture of their children's education, including the Parents' Centre web site, Learning Journey booklets about the curriculum and an informal *Parents and Schools* magazine. With parent governors sitting on LEA education committees, these measures add up to a considerable package of parental rights to information and involvement and partnership in the direction of children's education. The issue is whether these partnerships are sufficient to palliate anxieties that parents may have in relation to the State's role in educating their children, and their own diminishing autonomy (Henricson, 2003).

Generally, the development of partnerships with parents has not impinged on the facilitation of open futures for children. Some of the provisions are geared towards enhancing parents' input into educating their children and ensuring that children benefit from compulsory education. The clampdown on truancy through parenting contracts and orders, as well as the encouragement of parental engagement with home learning, are examples here. Furthermore, parental autonomy has been diminished in recent years in order to reach children directly with support. For example, there has been a substantial expansion in personal, social and health education in schools. Many of the functions that parents might have thought were their responsibility – such as talking about the role of marriage, the nature and responsibilities of good parenting, sex and relationship education, self-esteem, self-discipline and respect for others – are now being provided by schools through this route. Furthermore, pilots have been conducted in schools to provide health advice and contraception directly to children on a confidential basis. Less controversially,

Connexions also provides personal development advice, support and opportunities directly to children aged 13–19.

Religion

Religious education is perhaps the most sensitive area where the Government has input into children's development and where it has to navigate between parents' wishes and children's futures. How has it coped in a country that has lurched from monocultural Christian traditions, albeit with denominational feuds, to multiculturism encompassing an array of religions and a swathe of secular perspectives?

Certainly there have been substantial moves since the 1944 Education Act, with its expectation of daily Christian worship and Christian religious education. The daily act of worship has been modified, and is likely to be reduced to a monthly event following a report by David Bell, the Chief Inspector of Schools, highlighting its impracticalities and constant flouting (Bell, 2004). Bell nevertheless proposes that the Christian nature of this worship should be retained. Moves to multireligious perspectives are more in evidence in religious education. Religious education (RE) nowadays no longer promotes pupil morality through Christian nurture. It is an exercise in the academic study of world religions. Pupils are not expected to adhere to a particular religion, but to gain moral insight through this overview of intercultural faith. As well as a moral justification for this approach, there is also a significant social one, the intention being to enable young people to participate with understanding in a society of diverse cultures. Even France, with its treasured heritage of secular education, is moving in this direction as it considers increasing the study of religions in its schools to foster multicultural understanding post 11 September (Debray, 2002).

There are, however, legitimate reservations about RE as it currently stands. The Institute of Education and the British

Humanist Association have expressed concerns over its preoccupation with six world religions to the exclusion of others and secular moral teaching. There is a tendency to avoid critiquing the religions, in deference to parental belief systems. This absence of critical appraisal does not equip pupils to explore and develop through rational analysis their own systems of morality and conviction. Empathy is fostered at the expense of fostering evaluative faculties (Hand, 2004; Mason, 2004). Advocating a shift in RE in favour of evaluation, Hand suggests that pupils should be:

> ... actively encouraged to question the religious beliefs they bring with them into the classroom, not so that they are better able to defend or rationalise them, but so that they are genuinely free to adopt whatever position on religious matters they judge to be best supported by the evidence.
>
> (Hand, 2004)

Scotland perhaps offers a model more conducive to critical moral and spiritual development. Eschewing assent to Christianity, the Miller report (Scottish Education Department, 1972) recommends that religious and moral education (RME) should provide for a process of personal search:

> ... it should aim to develop a child's awareness of self and others, an insight into situations which pose moral and religious questions, and a capacity to respond to these situations in a balanced and understanding way.
>
> (Brown, 2004)

In its final implementation, RME included 'Christianity, World Religions and Personal Search'. There has been a significant shift towards critical analysis in Scottish schools and there are currently moves to enhance further the role of personal search.

It is hard to see how religious schools, which parents may choose to send their children to, fit into this scheme of multifaith curricula. They are part of the tradition of education in the UK as secularism is in France, and certainly they are permissible under international protocols. But the degree to which they are conducive to providing children with open futures must be questionable, and the Government's continued support of them is somewhat incongruous juxtaposed with its moves in RE to support multi- rather than single-faith pedagogy. Complaints have been made over exclusive statutory support for Christian foundations, and efforts are now being made to support other faith schools. This greater even-handedness is welcome. However, the question marks over the funding of faith schools, of whatever religious persuasion, remain because these schools are unlikely by their very nature to be the optimum venues for providing children with open spiritual futures.

Children's voice
Throughout the dynamic interplay in education between child welfare and parental engagement, one can detect a significant failure on the part of the Government to accord sufficient space to children's views. The child's perspective is absent from school choice and receives scant recognition in school governance. It is parents and not children who determine participation in RE and personal, social and health education.

This has been widely and adversely commented on by children's rights analysts in the field. Monk (2002) writes of an 'almost total absence of legal recognition of children's rights in education'; Freeman (1996) notes their neglect in the Education

Acts, many of which take cognisance of parents' agency and role in selecting and participating in the development of schools' policies. The main piece of legislation introduced by the New Labour administration underwriting education, the School Standards and Framework Act 1998, focused on standards and planning, and while, arguably, children were the beneficiaries of these, children's rights did not feature. While the Government has recognised in principle the need to ascertain the views of young people about the education decisions that affect their lives, with some realisation of this in assessing special needs, there has been no further significant statutory provision supporting such an approach (Monk, 2002).

The issue becomes particularly pertinent in relation to older children with the mental capacity to make judgements in relation to school choice, continued attendance and withdrawal from sex and religious education, and in respect of which conflicts of interest may arise with their parents. The failure to invest a degree of educational autonomy and discretion in mature adolescents is perverse and counter to their rights established in the medical sphere by the Gillick case (Meredith, 2001).

It also runs counter to international stipulation. The UN Committee on the Rights of the Child (2002) expressed concerns in its report on the UK over the absence of systematic consultation with children in education. Specifically, children's views should be gauged in respect of discipline. Some level of say in their destinies is not only a right but also important for children's education, so that they gain experience in being active citizens participating in the life and decisions of their community.

Criminal responsibility

Youth justice has been one of the Government's flagship social programmes with the establishment of multiagency Youth

Offending Teams and the Youth Justice Board, and the introduction of the Crime and Disorder Act 1998 and Anti-social Behaviour Act 2003, but, in the face of the criticisms it has drawn from children and parenting organisations, has this policy turned into something of a quagmire? The Government has sought to tighten personal responsibility across the generations, giving rise to anxiety among those engaged in child and family support who consider the approach overly punitive.

It has sought to enhance children's agency in relation to criminal activity, while at the same time reinforcing parents' role in managing their children's behaviour. Are these two propositions compatible? Probably in an imprecise world they are; the interplay between children's dependence and independence, child and familial determination, is fluid and overlapping. The question is perhaps, more critically, whether, in this complex world of human relationships, the Government has made an accurate and fair assessment of the point at which children should be held as legally responsible for their actions and of the scope of parental responsibility.

Children

The age of criminal responsibility in England and Wales is set too low within the rights framework of the CRC. Notwithstanding the Convention's promotion of children's rights of self-determination, self-determination does not tend to be raised in the context of criminal culpability for welfare reasons; children's interests would be ill served by drawing them into the criminal justice system at an early age.

The interpretation placed on the CRC by the UN Committee on the Rights of the Child led it to condemn the UK Government's promotion of childhood agency as part of its crime management programme:

The Committee is particularly concerned that the age at which children enter the criminal justice system is low with the age of criminal responsibility still set at 8 years in Scotland and 10 years in the rest of the State party and the abolition of the principle of doli incapax ... The Committee is particularly concerned that since the State party's initial report, children between 12 and 14 years of age are now being deprived of their liberty. More generally, the Committee is deeply concerned at the increasing numbers of children in custody, at earlier ages for lesser offences, and for longer custodial sentences imposed by the recent increased court powers to give detention and training orders. Therefore, it is the concern of the Committee that deprivation of liberty is not being used only as a measure of last resort and for the shortest appropriate period of time, in violation of article 37 (b) of the convention.

(UN Committee on the Rights of the Child, 2002)

The House of Lords and House of Commons Joint Committee on Human Rights (2003) has endorsed these criticisms, expressing concerns that the Government's punitive approach is causing it to breach Articles 37 and 40 of the CRC.

The relationship between State and child appears to have gone somewhat awry in the criminal justice context. Critics consider the State's protective obligations supporting children's welfare are not being met, with adult status being thrust on children too early and children's agency in this instance being taken too far. Certainly these arguments holding the Government's position in question are potent. There is no evidence, for example, that children are more precocious in the UK than in other parts of Europe where the age of criminal responsibility is higher. There is default of the UK's obligations under the CRC, which is not mirrored in comparable European jurisdictions.

Parents

While the age of criminal responsibility is based on excessive assumptions about the extent of children's agency and independence, the attribution of blame to parents for their children's conduct up to the age of 16 underestimates that level of independence. And, as with the issue of children's culpability and treatment in the criminal justice system, it could contravene international obligations.

The cause célèbre in the Government's project to enhance parental responsibility has been the parenting order. While parents may be supported by schools, youth justice workers and other agencies, there can be no doubt from recent legislation and pronouncements that the Government attributes primary responsibility for controlling children's behaviour to parents. The 'parenting order' is an outstanding exemplar of this. Brought in by the Crime and Disorder Act 1998, it gives magistrates the opportunity, where a child has committed an offence or has truanted, of directing the parent to engage in some form of guidance or counselling.

Despite the supportive thrust of parenting orders, there was an outcry among family and children's organisations and in the youth justice field when they were introduced. An array of arguments were marshalled against holding parents responsible for their children's behaviour in this way. They ranged from doubts around the efficiency of compulsion to legal and human rights considerations arising from the attribution of blame for the conduct of one person to another; parents would in effect be criminalised without having committed a crime.

An evaluation of parenting orders has found that, despite initial resentment over compulsion, parents who have been subject to them have themselves perceived a benefit from the programmes (Ghate and Ramella, 2002). On the deficit side, there are continuing human rights issues and concerns over the rather straightforward blaming of parents for their failure to secure positive behavioural outcomes for their children (Henricson, 2003).

Buoyed by the success of parenting orders, the Government has expanded their scope and the circumstances in which they can be used under the Anti-social Behaviour Act 2003. The Crime and Disorder Act 1998 has been amended to enable a parenting order to include a requirement that a parent should attend a residential parenting course. Arguably this is an erosion of civil liberties, bearing in mind that there is no qualifying criterion that the parents themselves will have had to have been engaged in any criminal activity. This human rights consideration may hold true notwithstanding the benefits that may be offered by a residential course or indeed the caveat in the Act:

> ... that any interference with family life which is likely to result from the attendance of the parent at a residential course is proportionate in all the circumstances.

Equally significant is the introduction of 'parenting contracts' and a broader reach in the capacity of the courts to impose parenting orders in the context of school. Parents can be invited to engage in a 'parenting contract' where their child has been excluded from school for disciplinary reasons, either permanently or for a fixed period, or has regularly played truant. If they refuse to sign such a contract or to comply with it, this will be taken into account by magistrates when deciding whether to impose a parenting order. And the imposition of such an order can be made on application by the local education authority (LEA) following a child's exclusion from school on disciplinary grounds or repeated truancy. There is no requirement here that the child should have become formally involved in the criminal justice system.

The parenting contract comprises a statement by that parent the s/he agrees to comply with specified requirements designed to improve the child's conduct (possibly involving attendance at a counselling or guidance programme), and a statement by the LEA or school governing body that it 'agrees to provide support to the parent for the purpose of complying with those requirements'.

Is it an equitable contract? Clearly, with the possibility that failure to sign could result in the imposition of a parenting order, it cannot be said to be a voluntary process. Furthermore, while parents' failure to comply with the requirements of a contract can contribute to the likelihood of a parenting order being imposed, there are no means established by which parents can enforce the authorities' side of the bargain, i.e. the support they are supposed to receive under the contract from the LEA or school to help them control their children's conduct. The Act specifically states that:

> A parenting contract does not create any obligations in respect of whose breach any liability arises in contract or tort.

While broader educational complaints procedures may be in place, there is no indication in the Act as to what redress a parent might have if the authorities fail to fulfil their contractual responsibilities.

The human rights issues that arose in respect of parenting orders under their first incarnation in the Crime and Disorder Act 1998 appear to be exacerbated by the new provisions to the point where they may be challenged.

Protective State

Faced with serious difficulties in containing anti-social, disorderly and truanting behaviour among some young people, the Government understandably wishes to make use of the tools available to it. However, with the current measures put in place to up and enforce the responsibility of both children and parents, it appears that the Government may have gone too far. It may be contravening both children's and parents' rights; at the very least it may have gone against the spirit of the CRC and the HRA. Both children's and parents' rights have been eroded – not one at the expense of the other on this occasion, but simultaneously. And has the State withdrawn from the equation? What of its protective function in these circumstances? It is perhaps a moot point. It could be said that the enhanced role of retribution and formal justice procedures undermines the State's holistic welfare response to children's and their families' needs advocated in the Department of Health's (2000b) *Framework for the Assessment of Children in Need.* This is not to underestimate the support mechanisms implied by parenting courses and the help offered to young people by Youth Offending Teams. But a culture of shaming and individual blame sits a little uncomfortably with the promotion of children and families' welfare as advocated by both the Assessment Framework and the CRC.

Overview of the above section on 'Self-determination and protection: the child and the State'

As we cast an analytical eye over the remedial responses to family breakdown and criminal justice, and the proactive role of education, what UK government policy threads emerge in relation to child and family policy tensions? Children protected by the State – specifically the child welfare principle – is a common theme, but there are gradations in the level to which commitment to this principle, established by the Children Act, the CRC and most recently by the EU Draft Constitution, is applied.

It is perhaps most constantly a guiding principle in domestic proceedings, although the mode of constructing 'welfare' still requires greater input from children's views and ways of eliciting these views need to be further developed. Broadly, however, it can be said that the child welfare principle dominates the operation of law around family breakdown to such a degree that it eclipses adults' interests. The right of parents to respect for their family life is relatively invisible and this is perhaps questionable.

It is also the predominant influence in education. We have seen the State supporting open futures for children and equipping children, sometimes at the expense of parental autonomy, with the wherewithal to participate effectively in a multicultural society. The intent is there, even if the delivery falls short. However, even in terms of intent, it could be argued that the Government has not gone far enough. Parents have some choice in the school they send their children to, but children have no official say in the matter. Parents have the option to send their child to a religious school, even against their child's wishes. And they have the option of removing their child from religious education and personal, social and health education. Religious education in the school curriculum has opened up considerably in recent years to address other religions as well as Christianity, and this is laudable. However, children are still not being equipped to challenge parents' perspectives through a critical analysis of religion and morality, and a process of self-search. Of course parents are their children's first educators and need to be engaged in their children's education, but in some critical areas there is perhaps the potential for greater support of children's individuality. Reflecting the sensitivity of religion, morality and parenthood, international protocols have some way to go in offering guidance here.

In criminal justice, insufficient weight is given to the voice of children who are offenders and, on the whole, their welfare is not the central point of reference. While the preservation of a safe society must be the principal objective of the criminal justice system, there are strong arguments for children's welfare being supported more effectively. The low age of criminal responsibility and the high level of incarceration of young offenders are matters of concern to those enforcing international children's rights provisions. Parents' rights, too, are not a significant consideration – witness the introduction and extension of the scope of parenting orders and contracts, reinforcing parents' responsibility to control their children's behaviour. The primary concern within the criminal justice system is the protection of the community. The challenge for the Government is whether it can provide that protection without eroding children's and human rights to the degree that currently appears to be the case.

Are government structures sound?

How often do reports on policy and service enhancement have recourse to structural change – management rejigging across the decks of the public and private sectors? Structural change is a tangible outcome that can be put into operation relatively swiftly and assuredly. But structures are themselves seldom the path to the full solution. There are other issues; there is the interplay of cultures, service habits, consumers, cash, delivery efficiency and more. With that caveat in mind, they can, nevertheless, have a significant contribution to make. They can be an enabling factor or a barrier to policy aims progressing.

From the premise developed in this report, the aims of child and family policy should involve the pursuit of a balance between policies that support:

- children as having a separate and distinct interest

- children in the context of their families

- human rights across the generations.

There have been substantial government structural changes on all three fronts in recent years stemming from dissatisfaction with the status quo and international pressures.

In terms of the international pressures, the ECHR established a range of rights for individuals – adults and children – enforceable in the European Court of Human Rights and now enforceable directly in the English courts. The CRC was adopted by the UN in 1989 to promote children's rights. It was tailored to address children's vulnerability with wider social policy implications than human rights instruments. Running alongside these developments were moves to increase attention to the child dimension within EU administrative protocols. Its absence from the EU treaties was found to be acting as a barrier to systematic incorporation of policy directives and standards to support the well-being of children (Ruxton and Bennett, 2002).

Approaching the issues from the perspective of the need to increase the efficacy of family services planning in this country, the *National Mapping of Family Services in England and Wales* (Henricson *et al.*, 2001) found serious dislocation between parenting support and children's services, with the former largely uncatered for in planning remits, and similar dislocation between adults' and children's services. The need for improved co-ordination of services was also cited in analyses of children's services planning by the children's rights lobby (Hodgkin and Newell, 2001), suggesting overlapping concerns.

Overcoming the barriers

National co-ordination

Responding to these concerns, in 2003/04 the Government instigated a massive overhaul of Whitehall departments with a view to bettering the co-ordination of children's services, drawing children's and family support together and giving both a significant boost. It has moved beyond an exclusively child-focused unit – the Children and Young People's Unit hosted by the DfES – where parents' roles were understated, to an inclusive administrative framework. Parenting support itself had been given fulsome treatment at the outset of the Labour administration with the strategy document *Supporting Families* (Home Office, 1998). But its champion was Home Secretary Jack Straw and a period of separate development ensued with children's rights fostered in the DfES, and parents' needs, linked in some measure to crime prevention, hived off, albeit making steady progress, in the Home Office.

This artificial division has now been rectified with the transfer of the Home Office Family Policy Unit to the DfES and its subsequent dissolution in a process of merger. There is also no longer a campaigning Children and Young People's Unit. Instead it is hoped that there will be a coming of age in a department with aspirations to integrate the processes involved in the government interface with children and families.

Other children's and family services have been brought into the DfES to complete the picture and to contribute to what is, in effect, a department for children and families, though the transmogrification has not taken sufficient hold to cause the department to change its name. The hard-nosed commodity of education still holds the nominal, and probably actual, rein; education is the predominant purpose of the DfES and it retains its nomenclature despite the creation of a Minister for Children and Families and a directorate of the same name.

Of the moves from the other departments into the Children and Families Directorate, perhaps the most significant is the transfer of child protection from the Department of Health. Although the move has given rise to some anxieties that health issues may receive insufficient attention, there are hopes that the transfer will result in a positive shift in focus. There have been concerns in some quarters over the pathologising of child protection responses in the past and their predominantly reactive nature (Cooper *et al.*, 2003). This may be modified by their relocation in a department, which, by its very nature, has a proactive ethos. Though, as they say, the proof of the pudding … and structures have their limitations.

Obviously, the whole of children and families' interests cannot be conjoined in one department; encompassing a substantial slice of the population's interests, this would rule out swathes of services delivered by other departments. After all, environmental factors, transport, housing, fiscal measures, criminal justice all impinge on children and families. Lines have to be drawn somewhere, but what is perhaps needed is a structural device to cross those lines. The Chancellor's domain, possibly with a smidgen of control freakery, has been the principal co-ordinating agency to date. But, with the inevitable preoccupations of the Treasury around slicing the financial cake, there are doubts as to whether some aspects of interdepartmental liaison are likely to be adequately accommodated by this route alone. For example, youth justice and health are areas where there is a significant interface with children and families' services, and the interconnecting issues are not simply financial.

In relation to the former, as we have seen, there are critical child and parenting interventions involved, and too great a segregation of children who transgress the law from the majority of children may result in a denial of rights and the adoption of an excessively punitive approach (UN Committee on the Rights of the Child, 2002).

Health, of course, has a huge input into supporting parenthood during its early stages through antenatal classes, health visitors and monitoring child development. There are, too, significant issues around children and parents' respective agency in determining the treatment of children that mirror those pertaining to the control of children's education (Archard, 2003). Then there is the critical relationship between adults' and children's health services, which is currently a running sore with a failure to address families' health needs holistically (Henricson *et al.*, 2001). Supporting disabled parents in their parenting role is a particular case in point. And there are important crossovers with child protection.

These are serious issues of co-ordination that need to be addressed. Interministerial groups have been used in the past and devices of this kind simply have to be made to work in order to bridge interdepartmental divisions that will always persist at some level. An interministerial group, Misc 9, has been established, but its powers are as yet unproven, and it will need to establish both a counterbalance to and rapport with the Treasury to be a significant force for cohesion. This might be facilitated if its remit were to encompass the production of an overarching family policy. Promoting complementary approaches, such a policy could openly address issues of conflict and convergence between intergenerational interests and rights within families. It could consider children's rights, child protection and family support, alongside issues of international as well as national regulation.

Local co-ordination

Restructuring locally has also been forthcoming post Lord Laming's inquiry into the death of Victoria Climbié in response to guilt and concerns over the mismanagement of child protection. Laming's report gave the impetus to moves that were already underfoot to counter splintered planning. Children's Trusts were being mooted to draw agencies together beyond what had been, on occasion, cosmetic planning co-ordination in children's services plans. Trusts were lauded as having the potential to overcome the divide between proactive support and child protection. Individual local authorities had been developing their own solutions along these lines, for example, by amalgamating education and children's social services. Children's Trusts, as introduced in *Every Child Matters* (HM Treasury 2003) and the Children Act 2004, are interagency administrative bodies designed to integrate key services around the needs of children, in particular education, social care, health, youth justice and Connexions. The Government intends that Children's Trusts should be rolled out nationally, following pilots, by 2006. With a view to enhancing accountability as well as co-ordination, the Government is legislating for the post of Director of Children's services accountable for local authority education and children's services, and for a lead council member for children.

Crossing agencies and mainstreaming something of a gaggle of recent government initiatives, the new arrangements for local co-ordination are impressive and radical, building on innovative developments by some councils that can claim the distinction of being one step ahead of the game. This unification of early preventative and reactive, hard-end protective services offers the structure at least in which a holistic approach to supporting children in the context of their families could develop. Of course caveats must be made; other support and direction from national government is needed as described earlier in this chapter, as is local will.

What might have given the inclusion of family services an additional fillip would have been to term the Children's Trusts 'Children and Family Trusts' – following the title of the Minister; explicit terminology can be influential over perceptions and possibly, in turn, over the direction of policy.

Rights

Moving from administrative hardware to a rights perspective, the question to be asked here is: has the potential via rights implementation to offer balanced support to children's and adults' individual and familial interests been realised? Here we have a half-full – or possibly half-empty – cup; progress has been made, but the Government appears perhaps to be reluctant to engage fully in the implementation of a rights ethos in family policy. Ruxton and Karim (2001), in their review of economic and social rights, note the reluctance of the UK Government to move beyond civil rights regulation.

The present administration must be credited with having brought the ECHR into a domestic legislative framework in the form of the HRA. The Act provides bottom-line protection for the civil rights of individual adults and children, and there are provisions for prospective legislation to be scanned for possible HRA contravention. Looked at critically, however, it could be argued that the Government has adopted something of a restrictive interpretation of human rights, focusing on contravention of the Act rather than also engaging in its promotion, and that this has resulted in a limited use being made of its tenets. We have seen examples of this in family law where the right to respect for family life fails to inform policy on contact and residence, and in the sluggish moves towards children being represented in family law proceedings, ditto parents being involved in childcare decisions. And there is arguably insufficient concern for the views of genetic parents under new adoption policies.

The opportunity for the HRA to inform the broad sweep of social policy has perhaps not been seized as it might have been. A new Commission for Equality and Human Rights is to be created amalgamating the Commission for Racial Equality and the Equal Opportunities Commission, and including within its purview faith, disability, sexual orientation and age. While this body has some potential, the focus of its remit will be on equality of access rather than service expectation. The HRA could possibly have been used more creatively to enhance the security and foundation of social welfare entitlements that are critical for the well-being of children and their families. There is even evidence of avoidance of social policy influence relating to the EU Convention's entitlement to education protocol. The Government has included a reservation in the HRA not to provide this right if it conflicts with the efficient provision of education to others or involves unreasonable expense.

The CRC goes beyond fundamental rights to address social policy overtly. The ratification by the British Government of CRC, but its avoidance of its incorporation into UK legislation, is perhaps again symptomatic of a reluctance to promote rights as the catalyst for enhancing social welfare on behalf of children. While welcoming the Government's responsiveness on a number of issues, the UN Committee on the Rights of the Child (2002) expressed its concerns over a failure to adopt a rights framework in the following terms:

> ... the Committee remains concerned at the lack of a rights-based approach to policy development and that the Convention has not been recognised as the appropriate framework for the development of strategies at all levels of the government throughout the State party.

These anxieties were shared by the House of Lords and House of Commons Joint Committee on Human Rights (2003) in its review of the implementation of the CRC:

Lack of a Children's Rights Framework

9　Likewise the Green Paper, a substantial programme for improving services for children, neither refers to the UN Convention nor to the Government's obligations to implement its provisions ...

11　In our report on The Case for a Human Rights Commission, we found that the development of a culture of respect for human rights is stalling and that the Government has a duty of leadership in this regard. The Government needs to embrace this duty, as we recommended, by a more conspicuous recognition of its obligation to implement UNCRC rights in its domestic policy agenda.

(House of Lords and House of Commons Joint Committee on Human Rights, 2003)

The UN Committee on the Rights of the Child called for the establishment of a Children's Commissioner in England, and, following the creation of Commissioners in Scotland and Wales, the Government embraced the establishment of this function in the Children Act 2004. But, by creating the role with a circumscribed remit, it has perhaps fallen rather short of the realisation of a rights framework envisaged by the UN Committee and other children's rights advocates.

The primary function of the Commissioner as conceived in the Children Act is to encourage account to be taken of children's views and interests, to advise the Secretary of State on these issues and to review complaints procedures. In promoting the views and interests of the child, the original bill stipulated only that the Commissioner 'may' rather than 'should' have regard to the CRC, although this was subsequently amended under pressure from lobbyists. The role does not have a judicial function and is unable independently of a request from the Secretary of State to conduct an inquiry into individual complaints.

Europe

And what of the anxieties that the EU has systemic deficiencies in promoting children's rights affecting the UK? Here structural progress is being made, but prospectively. As indicated in Chapter 2, the EU's Draft Constitution reflects a positive response to a children's movement that has lobbied for high-level policy endorsement of the normative standards of the CRC. Under the proposals, the Union's objectives support protection of children's rights, including respect for the principles of the CRC. In its chapter on Fundamental Rights, the Constitution provides:

1   Children shall have the right to such protection and care as is necessary for their well being. They may express their views freely. Such views should be taken into consideration on matters which concern them in accordance with their age and maturity.

2   In all actions relating to children, whether taken by public authorities or private institutions, the child's best interests must be a primary consideration.
(European Communities, 2003, Article 11-24)

These statements of principle are likely to have an influence on other EU instruments, resulting in the incorporation of a children's dimension across EU international governance. For example, Ruxton and Bennett's (2002) request for guidance on the incorporation of a children's perspective into National Action Plans (NAPs) is more likely to materialise pursuant to this creation of a European legal basis for the protection of the rights and needs of children.

Shortcomings

While the EU Constitution incorporates children's and human rights, and makes specific provision for the protection of the family and the promotion of intergenerational solidarity, what it conspicuously fails to do is to address head-on the possibility of divergent interests of children and their parents. This is starkly in evidence in Article 11-14, the right to education, where there is a provision that acknowledges parents' entitlement to ensure that the education and teaching of their children is in conformity with their own – the parents' – religious and pedagogical convictions. There is no consideration here as to how this parental right is to be reconciled with a child's right to be heard established under Article 11-24, or indeed any recognition that there might on occasion be a conflict of entitlement.

Concluding remarks

Europe's failure to consider intrafamily generational conflict and ways of addressing this in the context of the family as a symbiotic social unit is mirrored to some degree nationally in the UK. As we have seen, there is an absence of a government statement addressing divergent and complementary interests of parents and children in some major areas of government policy, such as education and tackling poverty across generations. The Government's recent radical review of children and family services administration may provide the integrated child and family structural backdrop against which such a statement could be reflected on and drawn up. The statement would add further strategic value if it were set in the context of an overarching family policy review.

The Government is to be credited with putting the blocks in place for coherent child–family policy development focused at the DfES, with a possible outstanding need for the pan-government committee on children's and family issues, Misc 9, to undertake a substantial role in bridging the remaining interdepartmental divisions. A meaningful operational relationship between this committee and its component departments, in particular the Treasury, will be critical if any real co-ordination is to be achieved. This is more likely to be realised if it engages in the development of a formally recognised, transparent and well-publicised family policy.

Arguably, on the lost opportunity side of the scales, is the Government's ambivalent attitude to a 'rights' approach to social, and significantly children's and family, policy. Rights have the benefit of long-term structural impetus, embedding entitlements within expectation and service delivery. The Government's diffidence has most recently been typified by its resistance to the social rights provisions in the draft EU Constitution. And, as we have seen, both the HRA and the CRC have been narrowly interpreted so that a rights dimension for the development of child and family policy remains elusive.

Summary

Poverty and the life cycle

1   There are EU and Council of Europe stipulations that place expectations on member states to address social exclusion across the life cycle.

(Continued overleaf)

2   The CRC makes recommendations for the redress of child poverty. In doing so, it identifies children's financial support needs with those of their families. It does not specify the proportion of gross national product (GNP) that should be allocated to redress child poverty in the context of different national economic circumstances. It might assist national governments if it did so.

3   The UK Government has taken steps to redress social exclusion across the life cycle (see Department of Work and Pensions, 2003a). The focus of the Government's social inclusion strategy, nevertheless, has been on child poverty, which it has succeeded in reducing in relative as well as absolute terms.

4   This agenda has been pursued from a welfare rather than a rights perspective. There has been closer identification with EU commitments.

5   In the interests of transparency, a policy discussion/ review is needed to develop principles and balanced policies relating to relative government investment in financial support for different age groups across the life cycle.

Family support and child protection
1   There is a fraught relationship between the Government's investment in early preventative family support and its investment in targeting children at risk.

2   The Government's Quality Protects programme and tracking proposals in *Every Child Matters* (HM Treasury, 2003) are indicators of its commitment to protect children at risk. The Government has also invested in early preventative programmes such as Sure Start, Extended Schools, Home Start, and the Parenting and

(Continued)

Children's Funds. An integrated approach between family support and child protection is advocated by the Government, and legislation and guidance favours keeping families together (Children Act 1989; Department of Health, 2002).

3   Although family support measures have been taken to comply with the requirements of the UN Committee on the Rights of the Child, 2002, there is little government documentation on family support that makes reference to the right to respect for a family life under the ECHR.

4   The Government does not, but should, provide an indication of preferred relative investment patterns across early and intermediate family support and hard-end child protection. This might be done in the context of a review of the relationship between demand and resources available for social care.

Self-determination and protection: the child and the State
Residence and contact
1   The ECHR and the CRC bolster children's right to be heard when parents separate. In the UK there are measures being taken, for example by CAFCASS, to ensure that the child's voice is heard.

2   The overriding principle in dealing with separation in the UK is the child's welfare. The ECHR underwrites parents' right to respect for family life, which has implications for contact. Although referred to in the Green Paper *Parental Separation: Children's Needs and Parents' Responsibilities* (Department for Constitutional Affairs *et al.*, 2004), it is not cited as a core principle.

(Continued overleaf)

3 A more balanced approach to international obligations would be to support parents in reaching agreements that maximise contact with both parties, subject to the primary consideration of the welfare of the child and the need to provide the child with a stable home environment.

Rights and education
1 Both the ECHR and the EU Constitution provide that children should be entitled to education, but also that parents should have a role in determining the religious and philosophical direction of that education.

2 Discourse on the role of the State and education suggests that the State has a legitimate locus in providing education that promotes children's 'open futures' and social welfare.

3 Religious education in schools has diversified to provide information about the six world religions. There are, however, outstanding concerns over the failure to include other religions, secular morality and critical appraisal in the syllabus. Government investment in religious schools is not conducive to children's 'open futures'.

4 There is insufficient consultation with children over education decisions (UN Committee on the Rights of the Child, 2002), for example in relation to school choice, to continued attendance or withdrawal from sex and religious education, and to discipline.

Criminal responsibility
1 The age of criminal responsibility (ten years) has been set too low within the rights framework of the CRC. The

(Continued)

welfare interests of the child are ill served by drawing them into the criminal justice system at this early age.

2   At the same time, the attribution of blame to parents for their children's behaviour up to the age of 16 underestimates children's independence and overestimates the ability of parents to control the behaviour of young people as they grow older. There are also possible human rights infringements.

Are government structures sound?
1   National co-ordination of children's and family policy has been enhanced by the integration of child protection, the family policy unit, and the children and young people's unit within the DfES. Interdepartmental mechanisms are needed to make the links with other aspects of government that affect families such as health, criminal justice, financial support and housing.

2   Local co-ordination has been enhanced by the creation of Children's Trusts, which are to be serviced by a Director of Children's Services and accountable to a lead council member. The integration of policy might be enhanced by renaming them 'Children's and Family Trusts'.

3   The Government has demonstrated an ambivalent attitude to a rights approach to social, and significantly children's and family, policy. Both the HRA and the CRC have been narrowly interpreted so that a rights dimension for the development of children's and family policy remains elusive.

4 Conclusion: THE ARGUMENT FOR A RIGHTS APPROACH

At a point of judgement – how far can one say that the Government has met the criteria of balance and proportionality in its dealings with children and families according to the criteria established in our initial examination of human rights stipulations? Balance, credence to adults' as well as children's interests, recognition of children's need for support and protection, the legitimate claims of the wider community – have the tensions between these multiple claims been addressed from a stance of considered balance and proportionality? And do policies in this area of both separate and convergent interests complement each other? The pattern that emerges can perhaps best be described as typified by pragmatism, a pattern that involves a juggling act from a beneficent perspective but without an established or transparent view of what the relationship between families', children's and community interests should be.

We have seen some moves towards endorsing children's rights. There are increasing expectations that children's voices should be heard in governmental service decisions. A Children's Commissioner is being recruited for England, albeit belatedly, and the Government has conceded to requests that the Commissioner should be under a duty to promote the requirements of the CRC. However, the tardy, concessionary nature of the Government's response denotes the hesitancy of its support for children's or indeed any rights. The Government's commitment is more clearly aligned to children's welfare with itself, rather than externally driven rights obligations, in the determining role.

Nowhere is this more clearly demonstrated than in relation to education, where, despite the Government's much articulated and genuine commitment to enhancing education services, it has placed a restriction on the human right to education under the ECHR where pupils present behavioural problems. More broadly, the Government 's lobbying to remove the social rights dimension from the EU Draft Constitution would have detracted from a range of rights affecting children, including education.

Across the age divide, the evidence suggests that the HRA and ECHR are not being taken into consideration in family and children's policy in as meaningful a way as they might be. They are not a significant point of reference in investment decisions and in the direction of policy promoting child protection and family support, in the involvement of parents in childcare and adoption proceedings, or in contact and residence decisions in cases of parental separation.

The laudable achievement of the Government in reducing child poverty offers a further indication of a welfare- rather than a rights-directed political philosophy. A rights formulation would suggest anti-poverty programmes directed across the life cycle, albeit targeted at points of risk. It would suggest the establishment of a minimum income standard and clearly enunciated service entitlements. These have not been established.

The absence of a rights approach guiding the relationship between the interests of children and families is significantly in evidence around concessions to that ill-defined attribution, parental autonomy, which in some circumstances one sees perversely preserved at the expense of children's rights.

In education, for example, parental choice of school and religious education for their child has been questioned as undermining children's rights. Mitigating circumstances might be adduced in relation to the former, in that choice of school is largely process driven to try to enhance school effectiveness through competition. Religion, however, remains a significant and emotive point. There are question marks over the curtailment of children's agency through the continued endorsement of parents' power to direct their children's religious education. Overall in education, the Government's role in the parent–child–State axis is to support children's individuation and opportunity for self-determination and fulfilment. But the relationship is seriously undefined and needs principled clarification.

However, it is not in educational choice but in discipline and control where children's rights are most seriously undermined. Retention of the defence of reasonable chastisement to the assault of a child by a parent remains a baffling violation of children's rights in deference to parental autonomy. And there are examples in the criminal justice system where children's rights have been undermined to such a degree as to bring censure from the UN Committee on the Rights of the Child, specifically in relation to the low age of criminal responsibility and high levels of child incarceration. Simultaneously, parents' human rights have been called into question by the imposition of parenting orders. In the criminal justice context the imbalance is in favour of protecting the community, and it is jeopardising both rights principles and individuals' well-being.

It is perhaps the slipperiness of a welfare approach that enables well-being to be undermined in this way. It enables particular preoccupations to dominate at a particular time, without checks against the rights of all interested parties. Taking the most difficult arena of mutual and opposing interests, family support and child protection, we have through *Every Child Matters* (HM Treasury, 2003) and programmes such as the Children's Fund a reasonably balanced approach; there are preventative supports for the family and complementary child protection checks, and a readiness through sophisticated monitoring to move into reactive mode when required. The difficulty arises as to whether this is likely to be sustained without rights stipulations. With decisions left to local Children's Trusts and service deliverers, the reactive pull of parts of the Children Act 1989, which place greater legal obligations on local services in respect of children at risk rather than children in need, will remain. The danger of scarce resources moving at any time in the direction of reaction is likely to continue as a dominant policy trait. Without a rights framework following the model developed by the European Court under the ECHR, which operates a tightrope balance between the rights and interests of children and parents, the possibility of slipping excessively in either direction is always there. One person's concept of welfare can very easily be another's oppression, and the failure to involve parents sufficiently in decisions about their children when the care system kicks into operation is a clear case in point where a proper appreciation of human rights obligations may require reform to existing legislation.

On the theme of population-wide financial well-being, we can see again the advantages of a rights perspective in regulating investment. Inevitably, specific interests will hold the ascendancy in the Government's and the public's concerns at certain times. If a welfare rather than a rights approach is currency, this may lead to investment being skewed in the direction of a vociferous lobby or an interest group with a hold over the public's sympathetic imagination. A rights approach would provide the yardstick against which fair investment over the life cycle could be judged, and, while this would include targeting groups that are particularly at risk, it would ensure that minimum and any aspirational higher standards would be applied to all.

Rights provide a framework and point of reference for handling interests. Interests sometimes elide, but also compete, and their reconciliation, or in some cases the championing of one side or the other, is the stuff of politics. Rights provide a pressure point and facility for reconciliation. They flush individual and collective entitlements out into the open. And they create expectations of a balance of interests that cannot disappear so readily as it might under a discretionary welfare model of government investment.

The UK has never had a family policy and the consequences are significant. The resulting void has been filled by a child policy where, whatever measures may be taken in support of families, they are done only in the context of a stated public policy aim of enhanced children's outcomes. Child policy cannot be equated with family policy because, by its limited, focused nature, it implies the eclipse of adults' rights, and many interrelated aspects of family life are not catered for, such as care of older people and adult interdependency. The nearest the UK has come to a family policy was with the Government's consultation document *Supporting Families* (Home Office, 1998) published when it first took office. No follow-up report has been produced and no family policy instituted. What has been established is a department of state and a ministerial group with responsibility for families, but the primary purpose of these institutions relates to children. Care of older people and adult services, for example, do not fall within their remit.

Quite properly there is a multiplicity of government policies. The advantage of adding yet one more – family policy – is that, while indeed it would overlap with other policies, it would provide a forum for recognising and reconciling interests that exist in close proximity and have the potential for friction. Children's rights and family support would fall within its broad remit. It would facilitate the development of complementary responses. With a primary function of balancing interests, such a policy would benefit in terms of direction and transparency from a set of principles to guide its decisions, and a rights approach, implementing the provisions of the HRA and CRC creatively and with conviction, would provide these.

Transparency is needed to promote collective and individual interests in a balanced and fair way. In order for distortion not to take place, and recognising the very strong pressures governments are under, that balance has to be clearly and openly cited and kept in mind as an objective. With a plethora of interests jostling for position, distortions may emerge inadvertently unless the process is monitored, and, because interests are difficult to reconcile, run deep and are emotive, affecting people's lives as they do, that monitor should be open to public scrutiny. What is needed is a statement on the relationship and tensions between children, families, parents and other adults' interests – intergenerational interests, and governmental measures to reconcile these, guided by a set of principles that adhere to international human rights, social as well as civil. It may not be a comfortable process, and would, as we have seen, imply some significant changes in policy emphasis. But, if left without the theoretically grounded steer of a family policy that adheres to the international instruments to which the UK is a party – the HRA, the CRC and EU rights – some of the social and legal anomalies that have emerged from this review will be set to continue.

Summary

1   A family policy is needed to provide a forum for recognising and reconciling children's and adults' interests. Children's rights and family support would fall within its remit. With a primary function of balancing interests, such a policy would benefit in terms of direction and transparency from a set of principles to guide its decisions, and a rights approach, implementing the provisions of the HRA and CRC, would provide these.

(Continued overleaf)

2 Rights provide a framework and point of reference for handling interests. They flush individual and collective entitlements out into the open. They create expectations of a balance of interests that cannot disappear so readily as it might under a discretionary welfare model of government investment.

Notes

Chapter 3

1 Another motive might be the cost saving to the State of adoption.

2 'Offers' in recent government terminology.

REFERENCES

Adam, S. and Brewer, M. (2004) *Supporting Families: The Financial Costs and Benefits of Children since 1975*. London: The Policy Press in association with the Joseph Rowntree Foundation

Archard, W. (2003) *Child, Family and the State*. Aldershot: Ashgate

Baker, H. (2004) 'MMR: mothers, medicine and rights', *Cambridge Law Journal*, Vol. 63, pp. 49–52

Bell, D. (2004) *An Evaluation of the Work of Standing Advisory Councils of Religious Education*. HMI 2269. London: The Stationery Office

Blair, T. (1999) 'Beveridge revisited: a welfare state for the 21st century', in R. Walker (ed.) *Ending Child poverty*. Bristol: The Policy Press

Boateng, P. (2003) All Party Parliamentary Group for Children meeting to discuss the forthcoming Green Paper on children at risk, 20 May

Brewer, M., Clark. T. and Goodman, A. (2002) *The Government's Child Poverty Target: How Much Progress Has Been Made?* London: The Institute of Fiscal Studies

Brown, G. (1999) 'A scar on the nation's soul', *Poverty*, Vol. 104, pp. 8–10

Brown, J. (2004) 'Religious and moral education: the Scottish experience', paper presented at IPPR seminar 'What is religious education for? Getting the national framework right'. www.ippr.org

Butler-Sloss, Dame Elizabeth (2001) 'Contact and domestic violence', *Family Law*, Vol. 31, May, pp. 355–8

Cabinet Office (2000) *Prime Minister's Review: Adoption: Issued for Consultation*. London: Cabinet Office

Campion, M.J. (1995) *Who's Fit to Be a Parent?* London: Routledge

Coleman, J. (1998) 'Civic pedagogies and liberal democratic curricula', *Ethics*, Vol. 108, No. 4, pp. 746–61

Collins, T., Pearson, L. and Driscoll, L. (2002) *Child Rights and the Family*. Discussion Paper. Ottawa: Office of the Honourable Landon Pearson, The Senate of Canada

Cooper, A., Hetherington, R. and Katz, I. (2003) *The Risk Factor. Making the Child Protection System Work for Children*. London: Demos

Cretney, S. (2003) Unpublished paper, Centre for Public Law, University of Cambridge, summarised in 'A policy for families' (2003) *Family Law*, p. 918

Debray, R. (2002) *L'enseignement du Fait Religieux dans L'école Laique*. Paris: Éditions Odile Jacob

Department for Constitutional Affairs, Department for Education and Skills and Department for Trade and Industry (2004) *Parental Separation: Children's Needs and Parents' Responsibilities*. Green Paper. London: The Stationery Office

Department for Education and Skills (DfES), Department of Health and the Home Office (2003) *Keeping Children Safe. The Government's Response to the Victoria Climbié Inquiry Report and Joint Chief Inspectors' Report Safeguarding Children*. London: The Stationery Office

Department of Health (2000a) *Adoption: A New Approach*. Cm. 5017. London: Department of Health

Department of Health (2000b) *Framework for the Assessment of Children in Need and their Families*. London: The Stationery Office

Department of Health (2002) *Integrated Children's System: Working with Children in Need and their Families*. London: Department of Health

Department of Health and Welsh Office (1992) *Report to Ministers of the Interdepartmental Working Group, Review of Adoption Law*. London: HMSO

Department of Work and Pensions (2003a) *United Kingdom National Action Plan on Social Inclusion 2003–05*. http://www.dwp.gov.uk/publications/dwp/2003/nap/index.asp

Department of Works and Pensions (2003b) *Measuring Child Poverty*. London: Department of Work and Pensions

de Wizje, S. (1999) 'Rawls and civic education', *Cogito*, Vol. 13, No. 2, pp. 87–93

Drew, S. (2000) *Children and the Human Rights Act*. London: Save the Children Fund

Eekelaar, J. (2002) 'Beyond the welfare principle', Vol. 14, *Child and Family Law Quarterly*, pp. 237–49

End Child Poverty (2003) 'Government abandons pledge to end child poverty', press release

Euronet (1999) *A Children's Policy for 21st Century Europe: First Steps*. Brussels: Euronet

European Communities (2003) *Draft Constitution for Europe*. Luxembourg: Office for Official Publications of the European Communities

Freeman, M. (1996) 'The Convention: an English perspective', in M. Freeman (ed.) *Children's Rights: A Comparative Perspective*. Dartmouth: Dartmouth Publishers

Ghate, D. and Ramella, M. (2002) *Positive Parenting: The National Evaluation of the Youth Justice Board's Parenting Programme*. London: Youth Justice Board for England and Wales

Gutman, A. (1987) *Democratic Education*. Princeton, NJ: Princeton University

Hand, M. (2003) 'Religious education', in John White (ed.) *Rethinking the School Curriculum: Values, Aims and Purposes*. London: Routledge Falmer

Hand, M. (2004) 'What is RE for?', paper presented at IPPR seminar 'What is religious education for? Getting the national framework right'. www.ippr.org

Henricson, C. (2002) *The Future for Family Services in England and Wales: Consultation Responses to the Mapping Report*. London: National Family and Parenting Institute

Henricson, C. (2003) *Government and Parenting*. York: Joseph Rowntree Foundation

Henricson, C., Katz, I., Mesie, J., Sandison, M. and Tunstill, J. (2001) *National Mapping of Family Services in England and Wales – A Consultation Document*. London: National Family and Parenting Institute

Herring, J. (1999) 'The Human Rights Act and the welfare principle in family law – conflicting or complementary?', Vol. 11, *Child and Family Law Quarterly*, pp. 223–35

HM Treasury (2003) *Every Child Matters*. London: The Stationery Office

Hodgkin, R. and Newell, P. (2001) *UK Review of Effective Government Structures for Children 2001*. London: Calouste Gulbenkian Foundation

Home Office (1998) *Supporting Families: A Consultation Document*. London: The Stationery Office

House of Commons Select Committee on Health (2003) *House of Commons Select Committee on Health Sixth Report – The Victoria Climbié Report*. London: The Stationery Office

House of Lords and House of Commons Joint Committee on Human Rights (2003) *The Government's Response to the Committee's Tenth Report of Session 2002–03 on the UN Convention on the Rights of the Child*. HL Paper 187; HC 1279. London: The Stationery Office

Hunt, J. (2003) *Researching Contact*. London: National Council for One Parent Families

Hunt, J. and Roberts, C. (2004) *Child Contact with Non-resident Parents. Family Policy Briefing 3*. Oxford: University of Oxford, Department of Social Policy and Social Work

Kendall, L. and Harker, L. (eds) (2002) *From Welfare to Well Being: The Future of Social Care.* London: IPPR

Kilkelly, U. (1999) *The Child and the European Convention on Human Rights.* Aldershot: Ashgate

Laming, Lord (2003) *The Victoria Climbié Report.* London. The Stationery Office

Le Blanc, L.J. (1999) *The Convention on the Rights of the Child.* Lincoln, NE: University of Nebraska Press

Le Grand, J., Burchardt, T., Hills, J., Namazie, C., Smithies, R., Stewart, K., Sutherland, H., Piachaud, D. and Vizard, P. (2005, in progress) *Policies, Concepts and Measurement.* http//sticerd.lse.ac.uk/case/research/

LGA, ADSS, confed, ACEO, NHS Confederation (2003) *Serving Children Well – A New Vision for Services for Children. Submission to Green Paper Team on Children at Risk.* London: LGA

Lord Chancellor's Department (2002) *The Government's Response to the Children Act Sub-committee Report 'Making Contact Work'.* London: Family Policy Division 2, Lord Chancellor's Department

McGlynn, C. (2000) 'A family law for the European Union', in J. Shaw (ed.) *Social Law and Policy in an Evolving EU.* Oxford: Hart Publishing

McGlynn, C. (2001a) 'The Europeanisation of family law', *Child and Family Law Quarterly*, Vol. 13, pp. 35–49

McGlynn, C. (2001b) 'Families and the European Union Charter of Fundamental Rights: progressive change or entrenching the status quo?', *European Law Review*, Vol. 26, pp. 582–98

Marshall, J. (2003) *Children and Poverty. Some Questions Answered.* Briefing 1. London: CHIP

Mason, M. (2004) 'Can RE achieve the things it's for?', paper presented at IPPR seminar 'What is religious education for? Getting the national framework right'. www.ippr.org

Meredith, P. (2001) 'Children's rights and education', in J. Fionda (ed.) *Legal Concepts of Childhood.* Oxford: Hart Publishing

Monk, D. (2002) 'Children's rights in education – making sense of contradictions', *Child and Family Law Quarterly*, Vol. 14, No. 1, pp. 45–56

Moss, P. and Petrie, P. (2002) *From Children's Services to Children's Spaces.* London: Routledge Falmer

O'Quigley, A. (1999) *Listening to Children's Views and Representing their Best Interest: A Summary of Current Research.* York: York Publishing Services for the Joseph Rowntree Foundation

Rawls, J. (1993) *Political Liberalism.* New York: Columbia University

Ruxton, S. and Bennett, F. (2002) *Including Children? Developing a Coherent Approach to Child Poverty and Social Exclusion across Europe.* Brusssels: Euronet

Ruxton, S. and Karim, R. (2001) *Beyond Civil Rights: Developing Economic, Social and Cultural Rights in the UK.* Working papers of Oxfam GB and Justice. Oxford: Oxfam

Scottish Education Department (1972) *Moral and Religious Education in Scottish Schools (The Millar Report).* London: HMSO

Stalford, H. (2000) 'The citizenship status of children in the European Union', *International Journal of Children's Rights,* Vol. 8, pp. 101–31

Stalford, H. (2003) 'Regulating life in post-Amsterdam Europe', *European Law Review,* Vol. 28, pp. 39–52

Sutherland, H., Sefton, T. and Piachaud (2003) *Poverty in Britain: The Impact of Government Policy since 1997.* York: Joseph Rowntree Foundation

Swindells, H., Neaves, A., Kushner, M. and Skilbeck, R. (1999) *Family Law and the Human Rights Act 1998.* Bristol: Family Law/Jordan Publishing Limited

UN Committee on the Rights of the Child (2002) *Consideration of Reports Submitted by States Parties under Article 44 of the Convention. Concluding Observations of the Committee on the Rights of the Child: United Kingdom of Great Britain and Northern Ireland.* http://www.unhchr.ch/html/menu2/6/crc/doc/co/United20:KindomCO2.pdf

Warman, A. and Roberts, C. (2003) *Adoption and Looked After Children – An International Comparison.* Working Paper 2003/1, Oxford Centre for Family Law and Policy. Oxford: Department of Social Policy, University of Oxford